Praise for Blind Spots

"Blind Spots takes a very pragmatic approach for those seeking to better understand how emotions impact their financial behaviors. Steve understands investor behaviors having seen the consequences firsthand. This book provides a great resource for those seeking financial independence through greater emotional self-awareness."

EDWARD HORWITZ, PH.D., CFP, MBA, CLU, CHFC, FBS, CSA

Co-Author, Money Mammoth

"Steve Booren gets in your head. His examples of how we can be our own worst financial enemy really hit home for all of us. Fortunately, in his book, Blind Spots: The Mental Mistakes Investors Make, *he also shows how we can help ourselves to achieve our retirement goals. You will really help yourself by reading it!"*

DR. JOHN NOFSINGER

Author, The Psychology of Investing *and* The Biology of Investing

"I have found that exceptional financial professionals always have a disciplined process and philosophy on how to approach investing and achieving goals. Blind Spots *easily walks you through a thoughtful behavioral framework. Emotional maturity is such a critical factor for everyone, especially those who are investing."*

ANDY KALBAUGH

Retired Managing Director & Divisional President, LPL Financial

"Blind Spots *is a necessary and empowering read. Expertly written and deeply researched, it opened my eyes to what I may have always seen yet did not fully understand. This book gave me the insights I need to better manage my own finances and behavior. I am recommending it to my family, friends, and colleagues. I consider it an essential read.*"

LEE BROWER

Founder, Empowered Wealth

"*Steve Booren's new book* Blind Spots *ought to be required reading before any investor ever invests even a single penny of their money. Investors are always looking for an edge and/or the wisdom and knowledge to profitably, and safely, invest their capital. They read books, they study markets, they take investment courses, they purchase research, etc. Yet the one thing they almost always overlook is the most important of all, and Steve highlights it beautifully in his book. The investment advice to first know thyself is—in my learned but humble opinion—the most critical investment advice of all. As a money manager, associate, and friend of Steve's, we share a common understanding. As renowned advisor to the advisors Bob Veres so aptly once said: "the definition of an excellent investment advisor is one that has the courage and integrity to insist that their clients do what they ought to do rather than what they want to do."* Blind Spots *facilitates solving that problem better than any literature I have come across. Therefore, I consider* Blind Spots *a must read for every investor.*"

CHUCK CARNEVALE

Co-Founder, FAST Graphs

"With over four decades of experience guiding investors, Steve Booren has penned a second book on the topic. This thought-provoking guide teaches you how to recognize and address your "blind spots"—emotional pitfalls that can hinder your investment success. Regardless of whether you are new to investing or have years of experience, this book has practical insights for all. It's a book that you'll read and reread in the years ahead."

JIM PUTNAM

Chair of the Board of Directors, LPL Financial

Blind Spots

BLIND SPOTS

THE MENTAL MISTAKES INVESTORS MAKE

STEVE BOOREN

Blind Spots: The Mental Mistakes Investors Make

ISBN: 979-8-9867825-0-8 (hardcover)
ISBN: 979-8-9867825-1-5 (paperback)
ISBN: 979-8-9867825-2-2 (e-book)
ISBN: 979-8-9867825-3-9 (audiobook)
Library of Congress Control Number: 2022915539

Cover Design by: Philip Studdard
Interior Design by: Kyle Haas
Edited by: Jocelyn Carbonara and Kyle Haas
Proofread by: Jocelyn Carbonara

Published by: Prosperion Financial Advisors, Greenwood Village, Colorado.

To Marie, my biggest fan; my family who brings me delight; and my clients who I love to serve.

YOUR BOOK, YOUR WAY

PRINT	Thank you for purchasing this book. Additional copies are available at multiple online retailers including Amazon and on our website, www.blindspotinvesting.com
AUDIO	An audiobook can be downloaded at www.blindspotinvesting.com
VIDEO	Video interviews that further cover the concepts in this book are available at www.blindspotinvesting.com
E-BOOK	Download the e-Book at www.blindspotinvesting.com for digital reading and easy sharing.

Table of Contents

Foreword

It's been a pleasure having Steve Booren as a participant in The Strategic Coach® Program with me for over two decades, and I'm excited to have been invited to again participate in his latest book. While his last book, *Intelligent Investing*, focused on the strategy and "why" for investing, this book takes a closer look at the behaviors that drive investors.

In Strategic Coach®, we coach successful entrepreneurs on how to focus on what they do best and find great "whos" to do everything else. We help entrepreneurs to "think about their thinking" and get out of their own way.

Steve, in his latest book, can help you get out of your own way, ideally with the help of a reputable independent financial advisor.

THREE CRUCIAL POINTS

I want to point out what I believe to be the three main points of Steve's book. The first is that your behavior as an investor is every bit as important as the assets in which you choose to invest. Asset prices are always in fluctuation, thus providing every opportunity for investors to react to those prices. Choosing to react favorably, unfavorably, or not at all can make the difference between success and failure. You cannot control prices, but you can control your reactions.

Second, you must discover your "why" for investing. What drives you to save and invest? Only with a full understanding of your intentions and beliefs can you better understand why you behave the way you do. If you seek to better understand why you react in certain ways, you can work to improve your emotional strength and exercise it for better outcomes.

Third, there are many things outside of your control in both life and finance. Your efforts to better understand and improve your behavior encourages better results. Whether starting a business, building repeatable habits, exercising, or saving a little more, everything starts with your behavior. And like building strength through exercise, you should strive to "work out" your emotional muscles.

HOW YOU REACT IS EVERYTHING

As an entrepreneurial coach, my job is to educate, encourage, and arm entrepreneurs with the tools they need to be more successful. But no amount of insight or education is helpful if it is ignored. Similarly, repeating the same mistakes often leads to the same outcomes. In order to improve those outcomes, you need to look at the process that creates them.

This book demonstrates that it is much the same for investors. If you're unhappy with your returns or your financial progress, what needs to change? Sure, if the market only ever went up, we'd all be winners. But the reality of fluctuating markets means it is up to us to make the most of it. Our behaviors, and resulting actions, will determine how successful we are.

This is why a plan is so important: it removes the need to react to every changing circumstance so we can instead focus on the things most important to achieving our goals. Write down your plan, seek help if necessary, and commit to it. This will serve you well when circumstances feel overwhelming.

BUILD YOUR EMOTIONAL STRENGTH

As you know, markets fluctuate all the time. Without a plan and a knowledgeable and experienced advisor, it is very easy to react emotionally. The more you build and stick with a plan, the less you'll be subject to emotional reactivity. The less reactive you are, the more strategic and successful you can be.

Physical and emotional strength are not all that dissimilar. Building physical strength requires repetition, focus, and determination. Proper training and consistency lead to a healthier and happier you.

To strengthen your emotional muscles, you must first understand how to use them properly. Like lifting an overly heavy weight, trying to do too much can hurt more than help. This book will give you a better understanding of the areas in which investors struggle and why. It lays out behavioral misconceptions and offers ways to overcome them. But these are only exercises—it's up to you to put them to use. With consistency and repetition, you can build the emotional muscles necessary to better manage your finances.

THE WISDOM OF EXPERIENCE

Though I suspect this book will be read by both do-it-yourselfers and those who work with a professional advisor, it is important to ask yourself at what level you feel confident in managing your finances. Many of the lessons in this book are easily understood but take a lifetime to properly put to work. As Steve has often said to me, "Managing *investments* for over forty years has been challenging, but managing *investors* has been much harder."

Too often, we are our own worst enemies. This book lays out a way to understand and overcome the biases we all have, but it takes time and energy. Sometimes, the best question is not how do I do this, but who can I partner with to take this task off my list? This is why working with a professional can be beneficial.

Whether you are committed to doing it yourself or to working with an advisor, this book can help you know yourself and stay strong to weather the inevitable financial ups and downs.

Dan Sullivan
Cofounder and President of The Strategic Coach

Acknowledgments

A wide range of people have helped me shape the message of this book. First and foremost are my clients, for whom I have had the opportunity to help navigate storms, opportunities, sadness, and joy. Working with them has taught me more about investor behavior than any book or class ever could. Thank you for entrusting me with the management of your resources. It's an honor to be by your side for this journey.

I am grateful for the many industry and business mentors, some of whom I've never met. I am a student of those I describe as "industry transformers." I can only hope to meet some of these giants.

My business mentors include the person I believe is the most influential entrepreneurial coach on the planet, Dan Sullivan of The Strategic Coach. Dan has helped me for more than twenty years with his quarterly meetings in Chicago. Some of Dan's tools inspired those you'll find in the resources section of this book.

I am so grateful for my investment behavior mentor, Nick Murray. Following him for the past twenty years has helped shape my thinking about investor behavior and inspired many of my opinions on the subject. Nick, you are a blessing to the advisors who follow your wisdom.

Warren Buffett's footprints have led me in my investment strategy. I had the blessing of meeting Mr. Buffett in the 1980s at a Berkshire Hathaway Annual Shareholder meeting. He appeared to be a "normal guy" and a gentleman. Returning from Omaha that evening, Charlie Munger was flying United Airlines coach class, in the middle seat, right behind me! He gave his wife the aisle seat so she could have more room. Both are prime examples of gentlemen.

My team at Prosperion makes me look good. You are patient with my moods, amazing in serving our clients, and constantly deliver on our promise of Care Beyond Advice. I'm surrounded by angels!

Kyle Haas, our brand manager, has been my go-to: managing the writing, editing, design, and all the other things I throw at him. Kyle, you are the best!

To my family, I am so grateful for your patience as I've devoted so much of myself to serving clients. I love being a provider. I pray that I'm instilling the life lessons that will multiply through future generations.

My wife, Marie, is my biggest fan. Your grace, kindness, understanding, patience, listening ear, and wise counsel help me every day. I am the luckiest man on earth!

Gratefully,
Steve Booren

CHAPTER 1

Why Are We Talking about Behavior?

For the past forty years, I've spent most of my days helping people with investing. The conversations have been as varied as the people sitting across from me: teachers, doctors, lawyers, janitors, business owners, and people from just about every other vocation you can imagine. While their circumstances and needs are often unique, there is one aspect that remains consistent across generations, vocations, and wealth levels: behavior.

My experience has taught me that behavior is a far greater tell of a successful investor than nearly any other characteristic. Your behavior as an investor tells me everything I need to know about helping, or not helping, you work toward your financial goals. Good behavior doesn't mean pinching every penny or saving every dime. Instead, good behavior is about asking for advice when you don't know, heeding the advice you receive, and personally taking action or finding the right people to put that advice into motion.

Those who are students of their behavior—and of their mistakes—have the opportunity to improve their behavior and outcomes. Let me give you an example.

I met a gentleman named Ted at a conference in early September 2021. Ted has been a facility manager for a large organization for several decades. He helps maintain the building and equipment they use, ensuring it remains ready for the next event. Almost thirty years ago, he and his wife sat down with a financial advisor and sketched out a basic plan. This plan, presented in a three-ring binder, outlined a few simple rules—rules that if followed, offered a shot at a retirement well beyond what they thought was possible.

The rules were simple:

- Avoid debt
- Save in retirement accounts
- Don't be greedy
- Don't spend more than you make
- Diversify

Even after raising four kids, putting them through college, paying for their weddings, and generally "doing life," they stuck to those basic rules. Today, they have about double the money the advisor thought they'd have. They have choices, flexibility, and a lifestyle that will keep them comfortable for years to come. They asked for advice, listened, and acted. Their good behavior allowed the power of compounding to work for them.

This book is written for those who want to be students of their behavior. Maybe you've made poor decisions in the past: buying at the top, selling at the bottom, chasing a losing investment, or selling a winning investment too early. Maybe you've let emotion override logic and want to better understand why that happened, and what you can do to prevent it from happening again.

As a result, this book is for both the DIY group—intent on managing their own money with as few illogical and emotional hiccups as possible—and for those who work with investment pros and financial advisors. It's important to remember that while those professionals are paid for their advice, there's little recourse for them if you call them up as the market tanks, demanding your entire portfolio be sold. At the end of the day, it's your money, and you're responsible for it. Ignoring logic in favor of emotion can burn an investor, regardless of their affiliation with a professional.

My hope is that this book will help make you a better investor. You'll learn more about why we often behave irrationally when it comes to money. Hopefully aspects of this book will encourage you to question your beliefs, behaviors, and attitudes. In doing so, you'll not only better understand yourself, but what you can do to generate a better outcome over the rest of your investing years.

THE IMPORTANCE OF GOOD BEHAVIOR

I believe your behavior as an investor will impact your financial future much more than asset allocation, degree of diversification, or even security selection. How you respond to situations and react to events, and your emotional IQ, will ultimately dictate your success at long-term investing.

Behavior reflects emotions, which are like an invisible muscle, always at work. Exercising my physical muscles with weights or repetition allows me to grow them into something stronger and more adept at handling even more resistance. Your emotional muscles work the same way. Trial by fire and tough situations all help to strengthen your resolve, confidence, humility, and ability to keep a cool head in trying times. Whether that's a divorce, an unexpected death, a welcomed windfall, or a challenging disability, an emotional situation both good and bad will test your emotional aptitude. As the adage goes, *the hottest flames forge the hardest steel.*

Like physical muscles, one's emotional muscles are best exercised in specific ways. Without direction or proper technique, the benefit quickly becomes a safety hazard. We've all been in situations where we've let our emotions get the best of us—influencing our actions, words, even plans. Like those who yell at their waiter, untethered emotions rarely help to improve a situation and can quickly put people on a course for disaster.

Professionals are not immune to bad behavior. Reflecting on my career as an advisor of over thirty years, I've had my share of cringe-worthy moments, managing money for myself and others. One example came in the late seventies, early in my investment career, after reading that the US government was auctioning mineral land leases to private companies and citizens. Winning one of these leases entitled the owner to engage oil and gas companies, who would in turn try to unearth black gold. It sounded like an opportunity, but the auctions themselves were logistically difficult to participate in, so I attempted to find people with expertise in securing these leases. My thinking was that I could win a lease, then turn around and offer it up to oil companies in exchange for a royalty. Fool-proof plan, right?

My first mistake was hiring a company in Florida to help obtain the lease. Why I felt I could trust someone in Florida with oil and gas leases in Wyoming...well, that was a judgement error.

After a couple of conversations with a salesman, he explained that many of his clients had won leases in the Powder River Basin of Wyoming. Greed set in, and my original plan to invest $5,000 suddenly changed to $20,000, a significant amount of capital at that time. But I wasn't too worried. *I will soon begin winning leases, and it won't be long before cash flow starts rolling in from oil and gas revenues*, I thought.

Little did I know that this company was effectively running a scam. They had nothing to do with leases but were instead raising capital for themselves.

How did that work out for me? I lost 100 percent of my capital. What was my recourse? Zero.

Greed (which ties into emotional intelligence and behaviors) blinded my common sense. This loss did teach me a lesson, however, that I still put in practice today: *complexity can hide a lot of sin*. I learned a $20,000 lesson on *keeping it simple*.

Had I invested that $20,000 in the Standard and Poor's 500 (S&P 500), it would be worth over $2 million today—and generating almost $31,000 per year in dividend income, or about a 150 percent per year return on my investment![1] That is why I call this situation *tuition*—because it provided me with an education, *for a price*.

LEARN FROM YOUR MISTAKES AND DEVELOP EMOTIONAL MUSCLE

Experiences like this can drive you to depression if you aren't careful. But if you rewire your thoughts to change your behaviors for the future, the *emotional strength* you can build in these situations becomes the education you need. By paying this tuition as a down payment on your future wisdom, it will serve you—both in day-to-day life and in managing your finances. When you can look back on your experiences and learn from them to better manage current situations, you become much stronger than the person blindly allowing emotions to run their lives. The tuition paid becomes worthwhile.

Emotional strength involves more than just withstanding hardships or making mistakes, however. It requires reflection to understand your temperament. This includes knowing your strengths and weaknesses—what you are good at and where you

---

[1] This assumes a start date of January 1, 1980, when the S&P 500 was at 110.92. As of March 31, 2022, it was at 4,391 with a dividend yield of 1.41 percent. (Political Calculations 2006).

fall short. It also involves knowing your boundaries or limitations. Emotional strength, gained in this way, is the foundation of good behavior and arguably of financial success.

Knowing how crucial emotional strength is to an investor's success, the purpose of this book is to help you understand and strengthen your emotional muscles in pursuit of more productive and fulfilling behaviors.

At a high level, we understand how emotions drive investment behavior, but rarely is this discussion applied to an individual investor's approach to saving for retirement. The aim of this book is to apply a high-level understanding of behavioral economics to the everyday investor in an effort to better understand what influences their investing behavior, which in turn informs their investment decisions. Those decisions driven by emotions can much more greatly impact their returns than what they invest in.

My goal is for you to *improve your behavior*. This involves recognizing when you are letting emotion distort judgement, when either the emotion of greed or fear clouds your viewpoint. I want you to have good investor behavior. I want you to be a better investor.

Good behavior can lead to fewer mistakes and much better investment decisions, which in turn could lead to more freedom, confidence, and returns—making your money work for you and your family, possibly for generations to come.

Join me in this conversation on *improving investor behavior*.

CHAPTER 2

First, Know Thyself

WHY ARE YOU INVESTING?

Occasionally, we receive random calls from referrals or prospective clients. Recently, this one came in:

I'm a dentist, and many of my friends and fellow dentists are getting into real estate. There is a group that invests in local deals in our area, and it is easy. All I must do is write a check (no property management, no upkeep, dealing with tenants, realtors, leasing agents, etc.). What are your thoughts on investing in real estate?

This is a stark change from 2008–2012 when no one wanted to go near real estate. That's when prices were inexpensive and investing in real estate made sense. Today, with prices up significantly, that's no longer the case.

Before I addressed whether real estate investing would be smart for the dentist, I asked a few simple questions:

1. Have you maxed out your 401(k) or SEP/IRA?
2. Have you maxed out a "back-door" ROTH IRA? Note: This can be a smart move for people wanting tax-free compounding, who are excluded from a ROTH due to high compensation or maxed out 401(k) or SEP/IRA.
3. Have you paid off your high-interest debt?
4. Have you paid off your mortgage?
5. Are you funding your children's college?
6. Are you contributing to a taxable investment account and taking advantage of the lower tax rates on dividends?
7. Do you have enough cash for emergencies?
8. Do you have excess cash flow, meaning you spend less than you bring home monthly?

If the answer is "no" to any of these questions, then putting money into real estate or any other alternative investments may be unwise. Checking off these items first is smart for most savers, especially before investing in something for which they may not have expertise, experience, or what I like to call a "natural advantage."

This example illustrates a simple idea: understand your *why*. In fact, consider defining your **what** and **why** for each of your investments:

- *What* do you hope to gain from investing in that area, as compared to other areas of potential investment?
- Go one step further: *Why* would you choose that particular investment? What makes *it* worth investing in over all the other options?

In the case of the dentist, his *what* is that he wanted to invest in real estate for an easy, no-maintenance return. His biggest *why* was that he thought he should be investing in real estate, because his peers were, and he thought it would be easy.

- Can you describe the **what** for each of your investments?
- More importantly, can you describe the **why** for each of your investments?
- Refer to the Resources section at the back of this book for help organizing these ideas with the Investment Filter Tool.

Simply put, it's hard to arrive at your destination if you don't know where you're going. Many of our clients simply say *retirement*, but what does that mean exactly? In your head, do the words *relax, relief, travel,* and *enjoy* come to mind? If so, you're not alone. A study conducted by the *Journal of Financial Planning* found that of the 990 participants asked to describe retirement, more than half used a combination of just twenty-seven words. The top ten words—*relax, happy, travel, retirement, family, fun, success, freedom, money,* and *fulfilled*—accounted for about 32 percent of the words (Lee and Coughlin 2018). Parrots have a larger vocabulary.

But that's how a lot of people see retirement. The belief is that upon reaching a certain age (usually around sixty-five), retirement is an expectation—a foregone conclusion. And once retired, people will get to enjoy "the good life" of unlimited freedom, time, and fun.

But when I'm asked to define retirement, I do it a little differently. I think back to 1996. I was a younger man back then, intent on starting my own financial practice. After spending twenty years working for a large investment firm, I desired an environment where I *worked for my clients.*

As I made the shift, my paycheck did not come from a company in some far-off city; rather it came from my company. It came from my clients who paid me for my advice. A fresh perspective brought about the attitude that going forward, clients—not the big brokerage house for which I had been working—would be writing my paycheck. And if my clients were paying for my services, would they demand I wear a suit every day? Probably not.

So that day, I retired my two-piece suits and checkered ties to the back of my closet, only to be pulled out for weddings, funerals, or the company Christmas party. I retired that coat-and-tie look because it was no longer useful or necessary.

When you describe retiring something or someone that way—as putting away something undesired—it doesn't feel as good. Instead, focus on what you're retiring to. I was putting away my coat and tie so that I could enjoy the freedom of working with clients in my own way.

My point is this: if you are planning to retire, you should think about **what to retire to**, in addition to **what you plan to retire on.**

RETIRE FROM OR RETIRE TO? FIGURING OUT YOUR WHY

Instead of only using words that describe a passive, carefree, vacation-like existence, what if we started to think about a more active approach? Perhaps retirement can be an opportunity to explore a passion project—using the skills you've developed for a purpose that doesn't necessarily make sense to your head, but to your heart. What would it be like if instead of a thirty-year vacation, you took your skills and passion and put them to use? Odds are you've spent the last thirty-five years developing a particular profession.

In his book *Outliers*, Malcolm Gladwell says you become an expert once you have dedicated ten thousand hours to something (Gladwell 2019). Over a forty-year career, at forty hours per week, you'll spend about eighty thousand hours at work. If it takes only ten thousand hours to become an expert at something, you're Mr. Miyagi (master karate teacher from the classic movie *The Karate Kid*) with well over eighty thousand hours.

What if you applied that genius to something you really cared about? What impact could you make?

Now I'm not saying you must give up the dream of a more manageable workload, more frequent vacations, or spending overdue time with family. If you're feeling burnt out and need some time at the start of your retirement, by all means, take a couple of years and enjoy it. Kick up your feet and watch TV for a couple of hours a day. Visit the kids. But when the doldrums of everyday life set in, think about creating again.

Focusing on building your passion can bring two benefits:

1. **You'll feel purpose.** We believe in making work a choice, which is to say that you get to choose what you work on, with whom you work, and for how long. Work is a lot more interesting when it's in support of causes you believe in, or toward problems you find challenging.

2. **Your income may be bolstered later in life.** Credible surveys point to a scary truth: 15 percent of prospective retirees have no money saved for retirement. About a fifth of Americans have less than $5,000 saved. Of those with retirement savings, the average amount saved is $98,800, according to Northwestern Mutual (Northwestern Mutual 2019). With longevity increasing, thanks to innovations in medical care, you will likely outlive your parents. Americans don't have enough saved to live on, especially for thirty, forty, or more years. But a willingness to work (and collect an income) can dramatically impact the amount of money people need to have saved.

In this way, retirement becomes a sliding scale of sorts. On one end, you "have to work" to maintain an income on which to live. On the other end, you can "choose to work," and you are free to choose if you work, on what, and with whom. This is true during all stages of life and is arguably a much better litmus test for your retirement preparation than simply turning sixty-five years old. Many Americans will work well past sixty-five, but their willingness to save and prepare today will ultimately decide whether that's a choice or requirement. If you think about retirement as a continuation instead of an ending, it's much easier to flesh out your *why* for investing. It starts with a solid understanding of activities that you most enjoy, and those that drain you. I encourage people to consider this distinction well before retirement. I help my clients to make a list:

- The left column heading is: **if you retired today, *what activities would you stop doing?***
- The right column heading: **if you retired today, *what activities would you start or continue doing?***

Try the *Retire From / Retire To Tool* in the resource section at the back of this book.

Are there things you can stop or start today? In thinking about these two columns, what would be the benefits of starting or stopping? What would happen if you began those activities now? What holds you back from starting or stopping today?

Take these answers to your employer, team, or employees, and begin to make these changes.

- What would you stop doing?
- Why do you do it today?
- Why do you want to stop doing it tomorrow?
- What will fill that space that you used to allocate to doing it?
- What is the emotional cost of continuing to do this?
- What will you start doing?
- Why will you do this?
- How will you start doing this?
- What is your purpose for doing this?
- What joy do you anticipate this will bring you?

Helping others can be profoundly rejuvenating if you find yourself lacking purpose in retirement. It can change your mindset from one of hanging the suit up in the closet because it's no longer useful, to leveraging your strengths and contributing your value. Whatever your *why* ends up being, retirement doesn't have to be the end of something. With enough preparation, you will have the choice to define your retirement and go after your *why*—however it may look.

TURNING YOUR WHY INTO YOUR WHAT

With a firm understanding of your *why*—or why you want to invest—it becomes much easier to structure your *what*—which is how your portfolios can build toward your why.

In our firm, we think about investing for our clients—so we can help them work toward their *why* with the right *what*. Some people are interested in cash flow or income (money in and out), while others may be looking for price appreciation (long-term growth in assets). This is true regardless of how you invest (real estate, stocks, ownership in businesses, etc.). However, certain investments may offer strengths in one area and weaknesses in another. A further consideration is your timeframe, and when you might need to turn the on income spigot.

- Investing in the stock market, for instance, can offer price appreciation and dividend income

- Investing in real estate keeps up with inflation on average, making it a poor choice if you're hoping for price appreciation. Unless you're good at timing market cycles or taking on risk with leverage, such as borrowing money to make an investment, you may want to stay away from this. Leverage (as in leveraging the real estate market) is a two-way street, and it's easy to forget it works against investors when prices fall.

With an understanding of your *why*, ask yourself these questions to begin addressing your *what*:

- **How will I invest?** There are many ways to invest today. You can buy direct ownership of companies via their common stock, or through other methods like Exchange Traded Funds (ETFs), mutual funds, variable annuities, unit trusts, and so on. With real estate, you can buy and manage properties on your own, invest in syndicated pools, or invest in publicly traded Real Estate Investment Trusts (REITs). Taxes are also a consideration with each of these structures. There are near-endless ways to invest your capital. (How do we do it? You'll find our methodology in my previous book Intelligent Investing. Reach out to my office at www.prosperion.us if you'd like a complimentary copy.)

- **What are my risks?** A significant risk with private real estate, for example, is the lack of diversification. Essentially, you are putting your faith into a single region, city, area, type, and economy. It takes a decent portfolio of properties to gain any level of diversification, especially when compared to a basket of stocks. This holds true for those investing in the private stock of a company compared to publicly traded shares. Diversification and liquidity are essential items people may not consider. If things go wrong, these factors can make or break a portfolio. Know what you own and why you own it.

- **How does this investment fit into my overall financial plan?** Real estate is an investment, so it needs to be considered along with your other investments as part of your financial plan. You might believe that real estate helps to diversify a portfolio of publicly traded companies, since their values may not move in the same direction as the broader stock market. While this may be true, the headwinds of liquidity and determining the value can be problematic. Stocks, on the other hand, are priced every day from 7:30 a.m.to 2:00 p.m. MT. You can see, buy, and sell them—all from your phone—at a moment's notice. Liquidity can be an advantage as well as a disadvantage. The ease with which we can buy and sell makes the urge to act impulsively an easy itch to scratch.

- **What is my edge or expertise?** This might be the most critical question. What do you know about this area and type of investment? Any investor should be able to answer this about all their investments. Do you have expertise in this area? Do you understand precisely in what you are investing? If not, are you outsourcing this expertise to someone with the right insight, experience, or knowledge? Are their interests aligned with yours? This is one of the core tenants of my work as a financial advisor, to offer expertise and experience.

Questions like those posed by the dentist about whether to invest in real estate often lead to more questions with no simple answers. The key when considering *what* to invest in is to understand your *why*. Knowing *why* you want to invest in something will help you decide if you *should*. This simple principle can help keep investors out of trouble and on a better path toward the goals in their financial plan.

WHAT ARE YOUR BELIEFS ABOUT WEALTH?

As humans, we're assemblies of experiences. Who we are is defined by the circumstances in which we have lived, along with our reaction (or lack thereof) to those circumstances. Our belief system is carefully crafted over time and reinforced by seeking input that affirms those views.

We'll talk more about this later in the chapter, but in short, we like to be told we're right. The trouble is that over time, our belief system—including what we think is right—can lead to poor decisions, especially if those beliefs are built on ideas that may not be entirely accurate.

Whether it's politics, finance, or even something as simple as paying a little extra for organic food, it's helpful to dissect our beliefs to better understand why we hold them. Then, it may be helpful to challenge those beliefs that don't help us achieve our *what* and *why*.

There are a handful of common beliefs in finance, some of which are more accurate than others. Do any of these sound familiar to you?

- It takes money to make money.
- The stock market is rigged.
- The stock market is a casino.
- Cash is the safest thing to own.
- Investing is for the wealthy.
- In life, it's the haves versus the have-nots.
- As you get older, it's important to invest in bonds.
- You must work hard to make lots of money.

None of these sentiments are factual, yet many consider them to be true. This cognitive dissonance—the mental disagreement between what we believe and what is true—can be damaging to our long-term outlook on life and misleading in everyday situations.

For example, let's consider the first one: *it takes money to make money*. First, is this factual? Of course not. Many people have been able to start businesses from nothing. To *build something from nothing* is practically a founding principle of our nation (though a belief itself!). Second, is there some element of truth to this? Yes, there is. Thanks to the nature of compound returns, the greater the starting amount, the greater the total return (all other things being equal). That's simple math.

The problem is when a half-truth becomes someone's whole truth. If they wholeheartedly believe that it takes money to make money, they're unlikely ever to save anything. With nothing saved, compound interest can't work on their behalf. When they reach a point in life where they need cash, they have no savings to utilize.

This in turn reinforces their belief. After all, if they had money, they would have been able to make more money. But they failed to challenge their belief and accept that *having* money can start with *earning* money, then carefully investing it.

That example may be a little far-fetched, so let's consider one that's more commonly held by soon-to-be-retirees: *as you get older, the balance of your portfolio should shift toward bonds and away from equities.*

Is this factual? That's harder to say. How a portfolio should be constructed is more art and less fact. There are no hard-and-fast rules about what should or should not be in a portfolio at any time. So, what's the half-truth behind this belief? That *as someone ages, their appetite for risk should decrease to balance out their need for their savings.* No one wants to be without the cash they need to live.

The half-truth is correct; no one wants to be without the income they need. But the belief *in how to accomplish that goal* gets layered on top. Instead, this "conventional wisdom" may be misleading if we don't stop to consider it.

As I write this book, bond yields are at historic lows, including the ten-year treasury, which is presently yielding about 1 percent. Long-term inflation is about 3 percent (Trading Economics 2021). So as an investor, you can offer the government a $100 loan, and in ten years, they'll give you back $101. But by then, your $101 will only buy about $97.03 in goods and services compared to today's money. Does that sound like a wise investment to you?

Other good examples of ingrained false beliefs tend to come from those who inherited money, and the lifestyle created by someone else's work. Their meal ticket was their family DNA, as opposed to the work and creativity involved in building wealth by creating value for others. The concept of building one's own success is known as K.A.S.H. confidence: an acronym for knowledge, attitude, skills, and habits, which we'll discuss more in Chapter 5.

Those who rely on inherited money tend to have no concept of how money is created. They have no knowledge of how to create value and be rewarded with money. The money just appears, and they don't know how to deal with it. They understand that many people would like a piece of their money, which all too often results in less fiscal stewardship than perhaps it should.

In my experience, inheritors also tend to form unhealthy attitudes about money. They may use it as a form of escape or entertainment, but rarely do they respect the money as much as those who earned it. This lack of *ownership* tends to create poor habits—and an unhealthy mindset. Without a drive, a purpose, or even something as simple as work to do, spending money becomes an easy way to stave off boredom. But no amount of stuff, cars, trips, real estate, drugs, etc. can create *satisfaction*, which is the ultimate reward.

Another common attitude among people who *attain* rather than *earn* wealth is sudden internal reconciliation that they may not deserve what they've received. This often results in guilt. This deserved versus undeserved attitude leads to a feeling that the inheritor is undeserving of their success.

A PERSONAL STORY: WORDS MATTER

Our beliefs, emotions, and habits around finances often come from stories that occur well before retirement. Childhood is a particularly powerful time for shaping these parts of ourselves that respond to the idea of money—or lack thereof.

Words are powerful—especially around the kitchen table. I believe how you were raised and the messages you receive growing up can greatly impact your beliefs about money. I was raised in a financially conservative family that bordered on downright frugal. My parents were first-generation Americans emigrating from Germany. They had lived through the Depression. These experiences made an indelible mark on their lives, which they in turn imprinted on my brother and me at our kitchen table. We were always told: "work hard," "anything that's worth doing is we're doing well," and "be especially careful with money."

The kitchen table is where habits are set. It's where kids learn about money. If your parents had a scarcity mentality, it's very likely you picked that up from them. If they had good stewardship, there's a higher probability you do as well. If your parents were cheap or stingy, you're likely in the same camp. Those concepts are conveyed and taught at kitchen tables. Today, we even go so far as to ask clients to describe what it was like at their kitchen tables growing up. You can learn an awful lot about people from that question.

I recall my father giving my mother a $20 bill for groceries and a haircut each week. It was as though she received an allowance and needed to stretch that money while buying groceries. Seeing this as a child left a mark in my eyes, one I carry today, that often manifests itself as an attitude of scarcity. I must fight back an innate fear: *There's not enough in the world—not enough money, food, or resources. I need to conserve, save, and be stingy with my expenditures.*

The reality is far from that. Our world is one of abundance, but it takes a different lens to understand why and how to tap into it. This is a struggle I constantly fight. It's hard to be successful at anything when you fear it will cause you to lose everything.

Compounding my fear of money was a fear I'd never be good enough to earn my way to success. Once again, the words I heard held power. I also recall my parents saying I would "not amount to anything in this world." I even recall them saying I would "live on Larimer Street," then called Skid Row (in the sixties). At that time, Larimer Street in Denver was where the poor people lived; today it is a hot, re-gentrified, retail area.

I still remember their exact words about their expectations for my future: "You won't amount to a hill of beans." That seared into my brain and left a lasting mark.

I say this not to draw sympathy or encourage you to disparage your children in a reverse psychology attempt to inspire them to work hard in life. Rather, this is to demonstrate that we all have our beliefs. Some of yours are likely good, some are bad. But all will need to be dealt with if you wish to approach your wealth with logic and a level head.

Ultimately, my parents' words were the fuel I needed to build the life I now have, which means they were used for good to help me challenge and reshape my beliefs.

Beliefs are just that, beliefs. Many aren't factual; instead they are founded on conventional wisdom, herd thinking, or even anecdotal evidence you've heard from believable people. It's wise to question those beliefs, because they may be creating blind spots in your life and finances.

What experiences did you have at your kitchen table, and how have they shaped your viewpoint and fears about money? Do those views serve you, or do you need to challenge them to change your behaviors? Who have you observed and put on a pedestal financially, only to realize they may not have had the success you wish to emulate?

RECOGNIZING YOUR BLIND SPOTS

Our perspective is the lens through which we view the world. It is our personal way of framing everything we see, and ultimately defines how we react to what life throws at us.

But from where do our beliefs come? We rely on our past experiences and perception of reality to shape our current beliefs.

Often this happens automatically, unless we remain mindful of how we're influenced.

In finance, so-called "professional investors" often share their perspectives (albeit often too much), which gives us unparalleled insight into how people may presently think about a particular subject. At any given time, is the market overpriced? Underpriced? Is it a good time to buy? Sell? Just turn on CNBC, and you'll get a deluge of opinions. These are the questions investors constantly face—and attempt to answer.

Investors, in their attempt to remain current, may become exasperated by twenty-four-hour news networks and financial commentary. Despite their abundance of TV time, these networks never seem to form a consensus.

Why is it that seemingly smart people with good intentions can come to such different conclusions about the same reality?

Some fifty years ago, Nobel-prize-winning author Daniel Kahneman and Amos Tversky wrote groundbreaking material based on a central thesis: people's intuitive expectations are governed by a consistent misperception of the world. In other words, **people believe what they believe based on their perceptions, not necessarily on facts** (Kahneman and Tversky 1979). Let's look at a couple of these perception biases.

CONFIRMATION BIAS

Confirmation bias is one perception bias, defined as *the tendency to process information by looking for or interpreting information consistent with what you already believe.* In a disagreement, it's easy to point the finger at another and say, "Well, you're just biased!" But the truth is we all possess a degree of confirmation bias if we honestly look in the mirror. Where you get your news, information, and even relationships is biased in part by your political leanings, upbringing, religion, and a million other minute factors that make you, you. Because human nature shows a preference for information that agrees with what we believe to be true, we tend to favor views reinforcing decisions we've made. We want others to tell us that we've made the right decision. We prefer to hear what we already believe.

Confirmation bias represents a huge blind spot for investors. Consider our earlier question: are markets overpriced right now? The typical misperception is that as stocks get more expensive (rise in price), they become more valuable. Said a different way, people tend to want to invest more in companies that have seen an increase in their share price. In turn, this leads to more and more investors chasing hot stocks. Say you were fortunate enough to have bought Apple in the eighties. My guess is you likely purchased more over time simply because it's been a "winner" for you. That's confirmation bias at work.

I find it odd that we process price and value in all other areas of our life in almost exactly the opposite way. Think of an end-of-year clearance on cars and trucks, Black Friday, and even Amazon's Prime Day. In the consumption economy, whenever prices are discounted, we get excited and mentally feel the value of our purchase is higher. We lean into our purchases when prices go down.

When things go on sale, I go shopping—at least for investments! We apply this perspective to managing investments for our clients.

Yet investors tend to do the opposite. Cullen Roche wrote on his Twitter on August 24, 2015, "The stock market is the only market where when things go on sale...all the customers run out of the store." This behavior is driven by the misperception that as prices go down, the value goes down. Kahneman and Tversky were right about people behaving based on their perceptions, not facts. This is a consistent misconception of the world. **Selling your investments in companies just because the price is dropping is the ultimate error in investor behavior.** Yet it seems to be human nature to want to avoid or flee a dropping stock, and it happens over and over.

One of the best examples of this behavior is found when looking at the flow of funds, a measure of how investors and their advisors are allocating or investing their money over time. On February 19, 2020, the S&P 500 closed at a new all-time high of 3,386.15. Over the next sixteen weeks, COVID-19 hit the equity markets, resulting in a fall of about 34 percent in just thirty-three days. The speed of this correction is without historical precedent. The following fifty days saw the fastest and steepest bounce in American history. Yet, investors were net sellers of some $171 billion in equities and net buyers of $1.1 trillion in money markets from January through May, according to data published by the Investment Company Institute. The same data says there was about $4.8 trillion dollars sitting in money market accounts at the end of May (ICI 2021). That's a lot of cash earning nearly zero return. This was just one of the more recent examples of emotions run amok, fear driving decisions, and some everlasting choices and behavior that harmed many investors for a long period of time.

RECENCY AND EXTRAPOLATION BIAS

Confusing short-term prices with long-term values is a classic investor mistake. Judgment is clouded by the blind spot of our own confirmation bias. How well the asset has done under *our* ownership tends to be the deciding factor, which turns a blind eye to the bigger picture.

This mistake affects seasoned pros and new investors alike. In May 2020, billionaire investor Stan Druckenmiller proclaimed, "The risk-reward for equities is maybe as bad as I have ever seen it in my career." As the markets surged some 40 percent following COVID, his portfolio returned about 3 percent. He pronounced himself "humbled" (Pound 2020).

Even Warren Buffett isn't immune from blind spots, including confirmation bias. Historically, Buffett argued investment in the airline industry is foolish. He once said that if a capitalist were at Kitty Hawk, they would have shot down Wilbur Wright (Buffett 2008). Berkshire Hathaway accumulated some 10 percent of the airline industry in recent years, only to turn and liquidate those holdings in March 2020 at their low prices. Even someone like Buffett, nearly knighted for his investment acumen, may need investor behavior reminders.

Are stocks fairly valued right now? That's a wildly generic question with no clear answer, no matter when you read this. But as you consider whether to invest or not, take heed of your own blind spots and whether you're using confirmation bias to reinforce your beliefs and judgements. Consider different perspectives and arguments that may challenge your views. Ultimately, it's up to you as an investor to decide whether things are overpriced. Your perspective will be the deciding factor, so make it as informed and unbiased as possible, or seek the help of a professional who can offer clarity and a second opinion.

IGNORING YOUR BLIND SPOTS: AN EXAMPLE

They aren't called blind spots because they're easy to see. As a financial advisor, I have a front-row seat to client behavior and the emotions around money. A large part of my job is helping to coach, guide, encourage, and at times discourage clients from making moves that could hurt their long-term investment goals. Ultimately though, the final decision rests with the client.

Ken and Bonnie (not their real names) were (and I stress the past tense verbiage) long-term clients, and a retired couple. Over the years, we had developed a solid game plan and implemented our investment strategy of growing dividends. It was working well. Ken was a Vietnam vet with some time in combat. As a result of his service, he was impacted physically and emotionally and received a disability payment from the military. Now in his mid-seventies, he had battled cancer several times, and the fact that he was alive was a modern medical miracle. Bonnie chased after their grandchildren and tended to Ken.

We had helped them become debt-free—coaching them to pay off their home mortgage, live within their income, and pay off a few investment properties they had acquired. As diligent savers, they also had a $2 million retirement account, which was generating approximately $60,000 in income, thanks to dividends. Between this income and their Social Security, they were enjoying excess cash flow—more income than they normally would or could spend. They were in great shape!

But I received a phone call from them in early March 2020. The market had just fallen about 20 percent due to fears during the COVID-19 pandemic. They sounded panicked and wanted some reassurance.

I reminded them that the price of their portfolio was always (and always will be) temporary, and that the dividends in the portfolio were continuing to be paid (in fact, several companies had increased their payments in the first part of the year). Looking at their income, their dividend payments had increased. All the extraneous fluctuation was just noise. It was normal and expected. I explained to them that price drops are normal; usually every year or so, a sudden, unexpected decline happens. That's just what the market does.

Their portfolio was made up of great businesses with a natural incentive to be profitable, grow more, sell more, create new products and solutions for the marketplaces they served, and do things faster, easier, better, cheaper. In attempting to achieve that goal, those companies would strive to be more successful, make profits, and distribute a portion of those profits, called dividends, to their owners, like Ken and Bonnie.

They contained their panic for a couple weeks. But after a third weekly conversation, they insisted we liquidate their portfolio, which at that point was down roughly 30 percent in price from its recent highs. They just could not handle "losing" this much money.

There was no way of knowing it at the time, but the steep decline was met with an equally steep and swift incline. Had they not reacted with emotion, selling their stocks out of fear and panic, their portfolio likely would have been higher by the end of the year.

Reluctantly, we followed their request and promptly suggested they find a new advisor, as they had ignored our advice.

In September 2020, after the markets had fully recovered from the temporary decline, I received another call from the couple, asking us to reinvest their funds. Now keep in mind they had delayed and delayed their "pending" transfer to another advisor. We reminded them of our resignation as their advisors and suggested they find a new advisor to whom we would assist in transferring their assets. They were shocked when we reminded them of this, asking if they had been "fired."

Yes, indeed we had fired them and suggested they find another alternative.

Knowing yourself takes a level of insight and understanding of your own behaviors and blind spots. Ken and Bonnie understood that they needed the help of an advisor but ignored our advice when it came time to do our job. This simple error set back their retirement plan and erased years of growth from their portfolio.

It's never fun to be fired or to fire someone, but for there to be a good relationship between our clients and ourselves as their advisors, three characteristics are essential:

- They must *want* our advice.
- They must *follow* our advice.
- They must *appreciate* our advice.

Without these three principles in place, the relationship will fail. It is like a three-legged stool: without any leg, the stool falls.

Make it a habit to question your own humility, especially when things are going well. When difficult situations arise, be honest, open, forgiving, and remember to be a life-long learner of investments and behavior.

CHAPTER 3

Behavioral Economics 101

THE LOGICAL EXPECTATION

With a better understanding of yourself—including your reasons for investing—we can dig into the impact of the study of economics, both micro and macro, on "participants" of the economy. This material—the educational principles and understanding of economics—is important, because it forms what I'll call the *old-school* and *new-school* ways of thinking about behavior. This research helps us apply discoveries from some of the world's best economic minds to your everyday investing.

Let's first explore the old-school way of thinking. Going way back to the 1750s, we can find studies of how people spent or invested their money. At the time, money was widely considered for its *utility*. Money was seen only as a rational means to an end, a tool to be used for an immediate and expected outcome.

Over the next two hundred years, this concept was reexamined, and two additional uses for money gained acceptance: *expected utility* and *discounted utility*. I'll try to explain both complex ideas in an easy-to-understand way, but bear in mind there is plenty more to read about the subjects, should you be interested.

- **Expected utility** is a theoretical "sure bet." People will wager more money on a potential perceived outcome, rather than the likely statistical outcome. You're at the roulette table, and the number seven has been landed on five times in a row. Which number are you likely to bet on next? Statistically, the likelihood of the ball landing on seven hasn't changed for any of the games, but the perceived likelihood has, thereby skewing people's willingness to bet on seven.

- **Discounted utility** is a way of accounting for people's patience (or lack thereof) in finance. If I were to offer you $100 cash today or $110 in a year, which would you take? Studies have found that many people gravitate toward the immediate option, one that puts the cash in their pockets today. But that outcome isn't rational or logical. Why not wait a year and get an additional 10 percent return on your money? This type of behavior can be seen across a variety of self-deprecating behavior: gambling, smoking, drinking, overspending, etc. People like instant gratification.

These two concepts—expected and discounted utility—formed the basis of what would become the new way of thinking about behavioral economics. However, they were still firmly rooted in the idea that most market participants were wholly logical, rational, and robot-like in their approach when it came to spending or saving their money.

Then in 1979, two behavioral economists named Daniel Kahneman and Amos Tversky published a book called *Prospect Theory: An Analysis of Decision Under Risk*. This book sought to better explain how recent developments in cognitive studies might apply to economics. Primarily, it tried to show why people made economic decisions that were not rational or were "asymmetric." It looked at four key areas.

FOUR KEY DRIVERS OF NON-RATIONAL ECONOMIC DECISIONS

First is *reference dependence*. As human beings, it's hard to understand all the potential data points for something we're trying to understand. Off the top of my head, I can't tell you what Apple Inc. was trading at on October 3, 1998. Instead, we rely on our references: perhaps what we first purchased the stock at, or its price after a key product release. Our understanding of "gain" and "loss" is then anchored to this particular reference point.

In our earlier example of Ken and Bonnie, they anchored their mind on the value of their portfolio in February 2020, roughly $2 million. When it had fallen by $400,000, they convinced themselves they had "lost" this money and would never recover. They thought it would fall further, possibly losing all $2 million, or 100 percent of what they had. This is *extrapolation*, or looking at two data points and assuming that what has happened will continue to happen. To use their language, "By the end of the year, it will all be gone."

Keep in mind that the same error can occur if you make an investment and see the price rise suddenly, say 10 percent over the past week. *Well heck, at this rate it'll double in less than three months!* That is the mental error of extrapolation.

Second is *loss aversion*. For some reason, people tend to avoid losses at a greater rate than they seek gains, by roughly 2.25 times. Translated to investing, this means a loss "feels" roughly twice as bad as an equivalent gain, thereby encouraging people to overcompensate for perceived risk (Tversky and Kahneman 1992).

Ken and Bonnie suddenly had a strong level of loss aversion. That emotion, along with bad behavior, led to a non-recoverable mistake. They failed to recall that their portfolio had doubled in value in less than ten years.

Mistakes can be very expensive. Checking your investment portfolio value frequently, then noting mental highwater marks, is a symptom of loss aversion.

Third is *non-linear probability weighting*. This is the idea that when making a decision, people will over-weigh small probabilities and under-weigh large probabilities. Consider a plane crash. Statistically speaking, plane crashes are highly unlikely. Thousands of planes take off and land without issue every day. Yet, when one does crash, because of its unlikelihood, the story tends to make the news and seep into the minds of viewers. That's why when people are asked to identify the likelihood of a plane crash, they tend to offer a higher number. The actual likelihood of an American being killed in a plane crash? One in 11 million, according to PBS (Ropeik 2006). You're five times more likely to be struck and killed by lightning (NWS 2019).

Sometimes we see people "barbell" their investments, with half of their portfolio in cash, CDs, or some sort of bond-type investment, then the other half with speculative investments. The thinking seems to be *I want to have my safety net of risk-free investments (that actually lose purchasing power over time), and I'll make up the difference by swinging for the fences with these long-shot speculations.* This approach rarely works.

Fourth is *diminishing sensitivity* to gains and losses relative to a reference point. The person with a million-dollar portfolio may not care as much about a gain of $20,000 compared to someone with a portfolio a tenth of the size. In much the same way a second bowl of ice cream isn't as good as the first, our sensitivity can change. If the price of bread goes up by $10, we'll notice that more than if the cost of a new car goes up by $10, even though the increased amounts are the same.

These ideas encouraged some behavioral economists to reconsider the foundation on which their science had been built: maybe people weren't always as rational as one might expect. This idea would win a Nobel prize for Kahneman and pave the way for two additional Nobel prize winners in the same field, Robert Shiller and Richard Thaler.

"The purely economic man is indeed close to being a social moron. Economic theory has been much preoccupied with this rational fool," wrote Thaler in his book, *Misbehaving: The Making of Behavioral Economics*. Thaler took the ideas of Kahneman and Tversky and went even further, arguing that much of economic behavior is irrational (Thaler 2016). He would win his Nobel prize for "…incorporat[ing] psychologically realistic assumptions into analyses of economic decision-making. By exploring the consequences of limited rationality, social preferences, and lack of self-control, he has shown how these human traits systematically affect individual decisions as well as market outcomes" (Neuman 2017).

In short, people generally are not rational; we're irrational! And because we're irrational, our markets, economies, and so forth can also be irrational as well.

We'll look at some of those irrational human traits and their effects in the next section.

BEHAVIORAL BIASES THAT DRIVE FINANCIAL DECISIONS

With an understanding of how we *should* act, according to traditional behavioral finance, let's look at how we *actually* tend to act.

Through the work of Thaler, Kahneman, and several others, many biases and behavioral mistakes have come to light. As I've mentioned, I often have a front-row seat to many of these struggles as clients work through them. It often starts with an innocent question, something like, "The market has gone up a lot lately. Should we sell?" As reasonable as that question may sound, it's really not all that reasonable. On a long enough time horizon, the market has always gone up. Logically, it makes sense that the market has gone up. And logically, it makes sense that it should continue to go up. So why sell?

This simple question reveals a *behavioral bias*, an irrational understanding of what might happen next because of what has already happened. This is only one of many similar behavioral mistakes that ultimately lead to irrational behavior. A purely rational investor would not entertain this question. But we're humans, and our nature is one of irrationality. That's what the new-school way of thinking about economics set out to prove. Along the way, other behavioral biases that seemingly affect investors were discovered.

Research often focuses on changing the behavior of large groups, but I'd encourage you to see which of these apply to you as an individual. We're all susceptible to behavioral mistakes. That's what makes us human. But understanding and trying to prevent these mistakes will allow us to recognize opportunity and stick with it, even when our emotions might tell us otherwise. In the next chapter, we'll talk about recognizing and overcoming these mistakes.

ANCHORING

Our first behavioral bias focuses on how we react to a certain number when presented with two additional numbers. Let me ask you: Did the S&P 500 finish close to 5,500 last year (2021)? What number did it close at?

Now you might not know the actual number (4,749.60), but I'll bet the number you answered with was higher than the actual number. Likewise, had we framed the question "close to 3,500," you may have guessed a number lower than the actual one.

You see, our brains tend to prefer shortcuts. We try to glean information from the question asked and use that information to estimate an answer when we don't really know. By offering a number in our question, we anchored your line of thinking—to a higher or lower number—and subliminally suggested it must have been close to that number.

This concept is hugely important when it comes to investing. Rarely are stock prices directly tied to the "worth" of the underlying company. Instead, they trade at multiples of that value, based on the beliefs of investors on what the stock will likely earn in the future. Without hard data, many investors instead turn to *price action*, responding to questions/concerns like:

- What has the stock done lately?
- Is it on a tear?
- Is it dropping like a rock?
- I bought some at $10, and now it's $100; that's way too expensive to buy more.

All of these are examples of anchoring. You're determining whether to invest based solely on a recent number, or one that you've invested at before. Sure, you may have picked some up at $10 (smart move), but that doesn't mean that it's not "worth" the $100 it's trading for now. It may be worth more than that, making it a continued smart investment. The only thing stopping you from investing more, in this scenario, is your bias.

HOT HAND FALLACY

Humans tend to believe someone can be on a "hot" streak, wherein something is just working for them. Of course, this is statistically impossible. As our compliance people like to say, "Past performance is not indicative of future results." Our string of wins is just as easily, and just as likely, to end with a loss as to continue. Whether that's in gambling, shooting free throws, or picking winning stocks, what happens next is not at all affected by what just happened. When you believe patterns in the recent past will affect the outcome of what happens next, you fall prey to the *hot hand fallacy*.

Now I know what you're likely thinking: *I don't do that. I don't try to pick winning stocks. That's a losing game.* That may have some semblance of truth, but how do you go about picking the people to manage your money? When evaluating mutual funds, do you consider the fund's return over the last year? Three years? Ten years? If so, one of your selection criteria is based on the hot hand fallacy. That fund manager may have their worst year as soon as you invest. Meanwhile, the fund that hasn't done well over the last year suddenly makes the right call, and the return takes off. One's history of success may well be a factor in choosing to invest with them, but it cannot and should not be the primary factor.

An argument can be made that some people are inherently better at their jobs, which would contribute to their improved track record over time. That's true; some fund managers are simply better at what they do than others. But picking a winner just because they've been winning a lot lately is where people get into trouble.

The same concept applies to individual companies and/or areas of the economy.

"Technology has been on such a roll; I want in."

"Why?"

"Because it's been on a roll, duh."

"Any other reason?"

"Not really."

This reminds me of a client years ago who felt he had a hot hand investing in the gaming industry. He requested that we invest all his retirement dollars into gaming stocks, thinking Las Vegas and gambling were going to explode, and he would be the sole beneficiary. We encouraged him to reconsider all his options, including finding a new advisor.

A couple of years later, he contacted our office requesting to come back as a client. He explained his IRA had dropped in value by over 50 percent in the last two years. He needed to get back on track.

When you think you have figured out the markets or allowed your ego to get ahead of common sense, that's when investing becomes dangerous. It's important to understand *why* a particular company or sector is performing well, then make a decision based on the bigger picture.

You'd be amazed how many times I've heard stories like this from clients. They are prime examples of chasing—and of our next bias, the *bandwagon effect*.

CONFIRMATION BIAS AND THE BANDWAGON EFFECT

If you're not familiar with Warren Buffett's saying to *be greedy when others are fearful and fearful when others are greedy*, you should be. It's an oft-repeated phrase in finance, designed to encourage investors to zig when others zag, to resist becoming part of the herd.

As humans, we tend to look to other people to see what they're doing. If a bunch of people are doing it, it must be right…right?

Wrong.

Just like your parents used to say, "If your friends jump off a bridge, are you going to as well?" That makes a lot of sense for your parents' example. But it's a lot harder when everyone else is getting rich from that one investment or sector while you sit on the sidelines and watch it all happen. It takes a lot of conviction and courage to believe you're right and everyone else is wrong, but that's what it takes to shake off the bandwagon effect.

If the bandwagon effect and herd mentalities are the *fire*, confirmation bias is the *gasoline*. Confirmation bias, as we've already discussed, is based on the idea that we like to be told we're right. Invested in a stock before it took off? You were right. Voted for the winning political party? It's obvious how right you were. The news anchor on TV agreed with you that people who put pineapple on their pizza are an insult to fine dining? We should make you President with such great decision-making.

Everyone likes to be told they're right. And it's great to be right! The problem is when you allow your right decisions to affect your next choices. You may have picked a great stock right before it ran up, but investing more now may not be a smart decision. The underlying conditions have changed, and what once was a great price may not be that great anymore. Yet investors tend to "pile on" to the winners they've chosen, regardless of extenuating circumstances.

This is true for news consumption as well. One needs only to look at two of the large news networks to understand how confirmation bias is alive and well. Conservatives tend to gravitate to Fox News, liberals to CNN. They'd sooner watch paint dry than turn on each other's networks. But when we let this dichotomy continue to pull on opposite sides of the spectrum, it alienates those in the middle. Our desire to be right trumps our search for truth, or to understand the real story.

The number of clients I've had to "talk off the ledge" based on political reasons alone is too many to count. A great example is a client, Kate. In a recent call, she was distraught with the outcome of a recent national election. It was as though the world had just ended. Income taxes were going to rise dramatically, the economy would crash, policies in Washington would destroy investors, and the stock market would collapse.

We tried to have an intellectual conversation with her, but she instructed us to liquidate her portfolio in November 2020. Two months later, we got the phone call, "Put me back in the market." Doing the math, she realized she had missed out on about 15 percent in price movement, or about $300,000 of her portfolio. This is someone who was in her late sixties and could not afford these types of behavioral errors.

Yet, this wasn't the only mistake she made. She also spent

lavishly, continuing to borrow money out of her home equity. Now she feels like she's also entitled to a safe and secure retirement. At the end of the day, this behavior cannot be blamed on anyone else. This was her mistake, and she has only herself to blame.

Every two years, we have elections. Every four years, we have a presidential election, and inevitably, close to half of the population is disappointed with the outcome. Looking back historically, if you liquidated your investments when your side lost the election, you'd be missing out on nearly half of the market's appreciation, thus limiting the success of your portfolio.

All too often, people take a very short-term view of current events, including elections. This is shortsighted to say the least. Politics can be divisive and challenge our outlook on the future, but through good and bad, the stock market has chugged along. You may not agree with what's happening in Washington, but that doesn't mean the world will soon end. Don't let your political opinions alter your investment strategy.

ENDOWMENT EFFECT

The endowment effect is an emotional bias wherein people value things they own more highly than things they don't. Again, we like to be told we're right, even by ourselves. As a result, we tend to think the things we own are valuable, since it was our decision that led to their acquisition. If you've ever tried to buy a secondhand car or tried to sell those "collectible figurines" in your attic, you've probably realized just how far apart you may be, pricewise, from the seller. The "sentimental value" is in full effect here.

We sometimes see the endowment effect in play when a client inherits stocks from a relative. The client will often wish to keep these stocks, even if they no longer fit their risk tolerance or goals and objectives. These stocks are somehow *special*, which warrants going against logic and keeping what may be a bad investment.

Likewise, if they own a bad investment, they may want to keep it far longer than they should. Loss aversion is at play here, but so is an investor's pride. If they purchased a stock at $100, and it's now at $10, they'll wait to "get back some of their money"—aka, stick with a losing trade just so their pride doesn't take a hit. This line of thinking hurts them twice: first, the loss from the initial investment; second, the opportunity-cost loss from sticking with a bad investment. Although we're only discussing price in this example, remember that there's a lot more to determining a good or bad investment than simply the price.

SUNK COST FALLACY

The *sunk cost fallacy* takes the same line of thinking and adds more fuel to the fire. It's where the phrase "people tend to throw good money after bad" comes from.

Investors, upon making a poor investment, may continue to

invest even as the value goes down. After all, if they liked the stock at $100, they should really like it at $75. So why not invest more? Rather than consider the value of the investment at the new price level, they just keep adding to their investment and turn a blind eye as to *why* the stock may be declining. In part, this is to avoid feelings of regret. But the reality is that investors may be chasing a loss, and no amount of "bringing your cost basis down" will help that investment change course.

Alternatively, if the stock price appears to be dropping for no apparent reason, it may be wise to allocate additional capital to it. Your decision-making should be done in **isolation from the current price, not based on the current price.** In the words of Kenny Rogers, "Know when to hold 'em, and know when to fold 'em."

LOSS AVERSION AND RISK-AVERSE BIAS

Many studies point to this surprising outcome: people are likely to feel a loss at twice the emotional level as a gain. So when a stock they own goes from $50 to $40, that hurts at a more intense level than the happiness experienced if it were to increase from $50 to $60. This effect drives people to avoid losses at all costs, despite the potential for increased gains. It also tends to inspire panic when the market experiences high volatility. Investors see their stocks dropping and jump out, only to miss the inevitable upswing when sentiments change.

We also see loss aversion when zooming out. A client opens their statement and is upset that their portfolio has gone down over the last quarter, completely overlooking the growth in the previous three quarters. Regardless of how much their assets may have grown, they lost money. And no one likes losing money. But they've only lost money in one quarter. What about two quarters? The year? Any other timescale?

Loss aversion tends to push people into asset classes that are far too conservative to meet the needs of modern retirees, such as bonds. Typically thought of as a "safe" investment, at present these assets only return a fraction of a percent. Compared to a long-term inflation growth rate of 3 percent, they all but guarantee a loss of purchasing power over the years and decades to come. So why do retirees pour money into them? On their statements, the value never goes down. Payments are "fixed."

My first job, working at King Soopers, paid me $1.19 per hour. If I had to live on those fixed payments today, I'd be very hungry. Similarly, keeping an overly conservative portfolio because of loss aversion will likely cost you in the long run.

MENTAL ACCOUNTING

Mental accounting often comes up during conversations about budgeting. In our heads, we earmark money for different purposes:

buying Christmas gifts, fixing the deck, saving for retirement, etc. Each of these expenses may even have a dedicated account. Maybe you have a jar with a couple $1 bills and some loose change floating around your kitchen counter. That's the savings account for the next family vacation.

In our heads, we create mental gymnastics and move money around because it's fungible. In effect, we're trying to save ourselves from ourselves. But money isn't fungible. Money is money.

For example, we have clients who sometimes have high credit card balances on which they may be paying 15–20 percent interest. Meanwhile, they also have $10,000 in cash set aside for their next vacation. Logically, paying off the credit card makes way more sense—using the money to eliminate the interest payment every month.

But mental accounting touches on something else: that personal finance is often more *personal* than it is *finance*. Many times, logic will dictate an outcome that doesn't feel right to a client. Sure, having a mortgage for thirty years makes financial sense, given the low interest-rate environment we're in right now. But wouldn't it feel great to have the house paid off and the payment gone?

That's why we tend to go against the standard financial advisor's advice and encourage people to pay off their homes. Simple math makes common sense, but there's no simple calculation for risk. Risk isn't just measured; it's felt with your gut. What your gut says may be different than the math. In this instance, the feeling of being debt-free—of owning your home outright—is far more empowering than a few extra percentage points. Debt is a tool, but like all tools, it's important to use the right one for the job.

Yes, we've had clients who elect to invest their reserves rather than pay down their debts (automobile, credit card, or student debt, for example). They prefer to find the extra few points of return that these methods can offer. To them, it's a simple math equation. But to many, there's a huge mental benefit to being debt-free.

As a result, mental accounting can sometimes be justified, even if logically it doesn't make much sense. Therefore it's helpful to understand yourself and the reasons you invest. A better understanding of your *why* can help create a better outcome, regardless of what logic has to say.

CHAPTER 4

The Things We Can't Control

So far, we've talked about why behavior is so important and the impact it can have on your portfolio performance over time. Managing behavior is like building a muscle at the gym: repetition creates strength, and strength gives you better performance. By training your emotional muscles, you develop the strength and skills you need to keep your own emotions from derailing the goals you've established.

Before hitting the gym, it's helpful to know a few helpful exercises. Otherwise, you're likely to hurt yourself. That's why we outlined a few basic behavioral economic principles so you can better understand what to look out for and how certain behaviors may influence you.

But there are things to look for that aren't necessarily behaviors. If anything, they're triggers—external influences that can set off behaviors (both good and bad). These are the things you can't control but must learn to deal with if you want to find success.

Triggers are just that—they're an invitation to react (often strongly) to a set of circumstances that you have no control over. **Your behavior is entirely within your control, but these events will likely test your will, patience, confidence, and emotional strength.** For that reason, it's helpful to understand several factors you can't control in an effort to consider how you might react to them. Things like:

- Longevity
- Volatility
- Inflation
- Distractions

Like an exercise routine, the deeper your knowledge, the more muscles you can put to work.

LONGEVITY

When do you plan to die? Weird question, right? It's one that financial advisors must ask their clients. The typical approach to retirement planning involves spending down the portfolio, a lifetime of savings for a client, at a rate that will ensure they have enough to live on now and for the rest of their life. The hard part is knowing how many years a person has left.

If risk is defined as the potential of making a mistake, I believe the most significant risk facing investors and their retirement is judgment about their life expectancy or longevity. Live too long, and you're liable to run out. Die young? Well, no one really wants that. It's a variable few people like to discuss, so it gets tossed to the backburner with a "let's just say eighty-five and go from there" type of answer. Ask a client how long they'll live, and nine times out of ten, they say they'll die at the same age their parents did.

The problem with this approach is advancements in healthcare, education, and technology. I think most Americans significantly and consistently underestimate their life expectancies. Much of this is due to the increased rate of longevity.

Life expectancy is increasing due to innovations in vaccines and antibiotics; they have indeed caused our health to improve significantly. Stories of pandemic flu today are solved in a matter of weeks or months, yet just one hundred years ago it wiped out millions. Tuberculosis and polio were common in the early lives of today's seventy-year-olds. Today they are non-existent. Knee, hip, and shoulder replacements are common, as are cataract and heart stents, enabling people with worn-out parts to lead active lives— free of what used to be life-limiting pain.

When baby boomers consider their life expectancy, they're using the same measuring stick their parents used, expecting similar results. But healthcare advancements in the past thirty years have been exponentially greater. This creates a significant gap between the *estimates of how long retirees will live*, and *how long they actually live*.

More concerning is the combination of a couple in retirement and their joint life expectancy. Your plan will need to outlive both of you. It's like taking the same issue and multiplying it by two.

Data reveals couples live longer than single people. This may be attributed to caring for one another, socialization, and plain old love. Living for another gives purpose to your day. Rarely do people plan for and consider the life expectancy of a couple.

Education is also a significant factor in determining life expectancy. Today, a greater portion of our population is well educated. Educated people tend to have higher incomes, are more active, eat better, and are more in tune with their health. If education contributes to a longer life and isn't just a correlation, many more Americans may have even greater life expectancies.

Underestimating your longevity is a significant risk and can become a large financial problem, especially for those planning to retire in the next twenty years. Pension plans cover the life of the individual, but as those plans are replaced with independent retirement savings, will retirees be prepared? Social Security may provide a base of income, yet according to the data published on their website, it only escalates at an anemic rate (only 1.3 percent in 2021, 1.6 percent in 2020, and 2.8 percent in 2019) and inflation has historically risen at 3 percent per year. This means the purchasing power of your Social Security income falls in half in just thirty-five years. Live ten more years, say from eighty-five to ninety-five, and you might see another 35 percent reduction in your purchasing power.

According to a study from The Senior Citizens League, the

reduction in the buying power of Social Security benefits from 2000–2018 was 34 percent. Some of the largest cost increases during this period were medical-related: Medicare Part V monthly premiums (195 percent), prescription drugs (188 percent), Medigap (158 percent) and medical out-of-pocket expenses (117 percent) (Johnson 2019).

Living longer is a goal to which we should all aspire. With advances in modern healthcare and technology, the goal seems more attainable than ever. As such, we need to start accounting and planning for longer lives and the effect they may have on our retirement. Your investments should support you at all stages of life, whether that's sixty-five or one-hundred-and-five, especially when going back to work is no longer an option.

VOLATILITY

DOES TIMING REALLY MATTER?

Do you ever feel "the curse" of investing at precisely the wrong point? Like you invested too late, at the wrong time, or maybe you're just unlucky? You're not alone. It's a feeling I hear from investors young and old. For whatever reason, "luck" is never on the side of those investing their capital. Whether too early or too late, the "curse" seems to follow them around.

While that may sound hyperbolic, I've heard it all too often. While it may feel like the world is out to get you, the reality is far from it. Let's look at some of the data regarding long-term investing. One of my favorite story-telling charts is included here:

Exhibit 1: S&P 500 Returns*

	Number of Periods			Percent of Periods	
	Positive	Negative	Total	Positive	Negative
Daily Returns	12,343	10,916	23,259	53.1%	46.9%
Calendar Month Returns	693	411	1,104	62.8%	37.2%
Calendar Quarter Returns	253	115	368	68.8%	31.3%
Calendar Year Returns	68	24	92	73.9%	26.1%
Rolling 1 Year Returns, Monthly	816	277	1,093	74.7%	25.3%
Rolling 5 Year Returns, Monthly	914	130	1,044	87.5%	12.5%
Rolling 10 Year Returns, Monthly	926	58	984	94.1%	5.9%
Rolling 20 Year Returns, Monthly	864	0	864	100.0%	0.0%
Rolling 25 Year Returns, Monthly	804	0	804	100.0%	0.0%

This chart, courtesy of Fisher Investments, details the historical performance of an investment in the S&P 500 (Fisher Investments 2018). On any given day, the market was positive 53.1 percent of the time, barely better than the flip of a coin. But stretch that period out and the percentages improve significantly. At ten years, the market had a positive return 94.1 percent of the time. In all of history, the S&P has never had a negative return when held for a period of greater than twenty years. Think about that!

That tells us three important things when investing over a long time horizon:

1. Volatility is much greater on a smaller time scale. The quicker you expect your investment to generate a return, the less likely it is to do so.

2. Trying to "time" the market is a waste of time and generally a fool's errand.

3. The sooner you start investing, the more we allow time to work for you.

Another example I love to refer to was penned by Ben Carlson on his blog, *A Wealth of Common Sense.* His post, "What if You Only Invested at Market Peaks?" outlines a fictional character, Bob, who symbolically invests only on the days before the worst crashes from 1970 through 2015. For his example, Carlson assumed Bob would save $2,000 per year, and despite his terrible timing on the buy, he would never sell. Bob was punched in the gut repeatedly throughout his investment career. He invested at the dot-com peak, the great recession peak, and so on.

Clearly, no one could be this poor at timing the market, but the fictional exercise yielded an important outcome: Bob retired with over $1 million, despite having only invested $184,000 (Carlson 2014). Even with the worst possible timing, Bob's behavior as an investor proved fruitful.

First, Bob had a plan. He was a diligent and consistent saver. He never wavered from his savings plan, and even though he had hesitations about participating in the market, he continued to do it. Second, Bob allowed his investments to compound through the decades, never selling out of the market over his forty-plus years of investing and his working career.

Imagine the tremendous psychological toil Bob endured from seeing huge losses accumulate right after he made each investment. But Bob had a long-term perspective and was willing to stick with his savings and investment plan—even if his timing was "a bit off." He saved and kept his head down.

So, what can we learn from this example?

1. **Investing requires an optimistic outlook.** Long-term thinking often rewards the optimist. Unless you think the world is coming to an end, it's the optimists who are rewarded.

2. **Temporary declines are part of the deal when you invest.** How you react to those price declines will be one of the most significant determinants of your investment performance.

3. **The biggest factor in investment success is savings.** How much you save, how early you begin, and how methodically you save have a much bigger impact than investment return.

VOLATILITY, OR HOW I LEARNED TO STOP FEARING STOCK MARKET DROPS AND START SEEING THEM AS SALES

The fictional example was to illustrate a common misconception of investors: that timing the market is essential for better returns. The simple fact is that *time in the markets* often beats *timing the markets*. Bob's reluctance to sell, even after all the turmoil he had experienced, contributed significantly toward his goal. Even when the chips were down, he hung onto his investments. He also unwittingly diversified his portfolio, electing to invest in a broad market fund representing some of the best companies in the world.

Unfortunately, this isn't typical of most amateur investors. When volatility rises and prices drop, investors start to feel a little seasick. The first thing queasy people want to do is to get off the boat. This is precisely the wrong thing to do, and here's why. Apart from the obvious trouble of being surrounded by ocean, the idea that fluctuation is bad is an incorrect perspective. Volatility is the stock market's way of redistributing shares of great companies to long-term owners. When markets fluctuate, however, it's nearly impossible to divorce yourself from the emotional powers of fear and greed. Yet the price per share does not matter unless you're buying or selling that day. Other than some "entertainment value," daily fluctuation should be ignored.

"What makes stocks valuable in the long run is not the market. It is the profitability of the companies you own," said Peter Lynch in *Worth* magazine in 1995 (Lynch and Rothchild 1995). I agree with him. Over time, as corporations become more valuable, sooner or later, their shares generally sell for a higher price. Our contention is *you need to remember you own a piece of successful, profitable companies.*

When we experience moments of extreme volatility, investors tend to get anxious and fearful. **If you are a long-term investor who likes owning great dividend-paying companies, short-term volatility should be expected and tolerated, even welcomed.** If you do not intend to sell any investments for many years to come, why worry about what the prices are today? Short-term price declines cause many investors angst, especially if their investment decision was based solely on price or how "hot" a stock or sector was. That emotional heartburn is just one reason it makes sense to work with a professional who can help get you on track and keep you there.

Managing assets for the past forty years, I often feel I live in what might be described as *investment manager hell*. When clients are excited, almost giddy with enthusiasm about the markets and economy, I tend to feel frustrated. Moments like these usually mean my favorite companies are overvalued.

On the other hand, when they express frustration, anger, fear, or anxiety about the markets, I tend to get excited. This usually means my favorite companies are on sale. Remember that falling prices mean better deals. Sometimes the price drops so far and so hard, it's possible to pick up shares at fire-sale prices. Panic can be an expensive emotion for sellers.

Rather than get caught up in the moment, I look toward the future and what opportunities may develop for investments. This is investment manager's hell—loving "bad" markets and hating "good" markets.

When you work diligently to understand each company you may own as an investor, you realize the company's value is the sum of its potential future cash flow. The higher the current stock price, the more overvalued that investment may be. Likewise, the lower the price today, the more undervalued that company is. It may be a great time to increase ownership shares.

When prices are temporarily falling, rather than be fearful, recognize that you can purchase company stocks at lower prices. Try to make it a practice never to react solely to prices. A more in-depth, thoughtful approach is necessary to evaluate a company's health. Price should not be the sole indicator. We touch on how to do this later in the book, but for a more in-depth approach I'd recommend reading my first book, *Intelligent Investing*. You can request a complimentary copy on our website at www.prosperion. us.

How you think about market fluctuation and, more importantly, what you do about it takes discipline. Often investors let fear and greed override common sense or wisdom. **Don't be a victim of the market. Remember, the best time to buy products is when they go on sale.** Great investments, like great products or services, sometimes have price drops. When they come along, consider buying them, keeping them for a long time, and watching what that decision can do for you.

INFLATION

When winter arrives here in Colorado, it's time for soup. And no soup feels more familiar than Campbell's tomato soup. Just the name conjures a familiar aroma, a warmth in your chest.

Campbell's feels familiar because it's been an American icon for more than a century. Introduced in 1898, Campbell's tomato soup is an excellent benchmark for understanding the impact of the persistent enemy of all investors: inflation. For more than one hundred years, the size hasn't changed, but the price sure has. About forty-eight years ago, in 1974, the soup cost about $0.12 per can. Today, it retails for a little over $1 per can. That points to an average inflation rate of 4.7 percent.

Forty years may sound like a long time, but that's about the length of a typical retirement. According to the Society of Actuaries, a non-smoking, sixty-five-year-old male in excellent health today has a 43 percent probability of living to age ninety, and a similar sixty-five-year-old female has a 54 percent probability of living to ninety. One-third of today's sixty-five-year-old women in excellent health and about one in four men are expected to be alive at ninety-five (Fried 2019).

With innovations in healthcare and medical services and a more active retiree base, I believe this life expectancy number will only increase, as we discussed earlier in this chapter.

A longer life points to a longer retirement, which in turn means a need for more assets to prevent you from "running out." Simply said, if your income isn't growing at a rate higher than inflation, you are losing purchasing power. You are getting poor, slowly. The sign for this is when people say, "My income just does not go as far as it used to." Over time, prices keep rising, and your income doesn't. This reality hits people later in life, often when it's too late.

Consider these examples comparing common goods from 1974 to today:

Example Goods	1974	2022	Avg. Inflation/ Year
Campbell's® Tomato Soup	.12	1.10	+4.72 percent
1 Dozen Eggs	.78	2.99	+2.83 percent
McDonald's Quarter Pounder®	.55	4.99	+4.7 percent
Package of Oreo Cookies	.55	4.59	+4.52 percent
Kellogg's® Corn Flakes®	.43	4.99	+5.23 percent

The problem is simple: over time, things get more expensive. Soup is one simple example, but other areas are more concerning. Healthcare, housing, education—all have seen significant increases in cost.

What's an investor or retiree to do? That's actually two questions. First, what do they *usually* do? Second, what should they *actually* do?

Typically, investors follow an old adage of pouring money into fixed income as they age, believing that "fixed" is good. Fixed feels stable; fixed feels safe. But it isn't. Consider this: From 2010 to 2020, corporate earnings of the S&P 500 rose from $83.77 to approximately $162, close to doubling. During that same period, US household investors were net sellers of stocks and net buyers of bonds (Political Calculations 2006). Investors liquidated stocks that were increasing in value while adding to fixed income investments that paid multi-decade low rates of return. This action based on a financial fallacy means they were trading growing income for fixed income, precisely the opposite of what they should have been doing!

Over these ten years, dividend income rose 2.6 times, from $22.24 to $58.28[1], while the government's official inflation rate (the CPI) rose 19 percent. For the first time ever, senior analysts at the Dow Jones Indices expected dividend payments to exceed $500 billion, an increase of 6.4 percent in 2020 (Langley 2020). Think about this...one-half a trillion dollars being paid to investors in 2020!

Another way to look at this is what we call the *earnings yield* or *owner earnings*. If you owned the entire S&P 500, what would you earn on your money, divided by the price? For 2021, the earnings yield of the S&P 500 was 4.3 percent (excluding dividends). Compare this to a ten-year Treasury bond at 1.75 percent (as of December 31, 2021). You could choose to have a broad portfolio of companies with great people incentivized to improve, grow, compete with one another, and be better tomorrow than today. Or, you could loan your money to the US government and earn a

---

1 This represents a date range from January 2010 to December 2020 (Political Calculations 2006).

flat return for the next ten years. It seems like an easy choice. [2]

Earnings, income, and *price*—of that in which you choose to invest—are important to understand as you invest your capital. Growing your income over a long period of time is essential to maintaining your purchasing power. Don't be distracted by myths of what is risky and what is not, nor those who attempt to "time" the market. It can't be done. Understanding how these three variables work together is essential.

DISTRACTIONS AND DOUBT

Many people believe the stock market is risky. It's often described as a casino, using words like *crash, falling,* and my favorite Wall Street word, *correction*—meaning falling 10 percent or more from a previous high price. **My definition of a correction is a little different: a temporary decline, which is then followed and surpassed by an advance.**

I help people understand that risk is a permanent loss, or (more likely) the permanent loss of your purchasing power. While there are no guarantees, historically money has never been lost when invested in a broadly diversified portfolio with a long enough time horizon. You must be willing to hold this well-diversified portfolio of quality equities through their normal, sometimes frequent, short-term declines.

---

2 The 4.3 percent average annualized yield represents all stocks in the index. Indices cannot be invested into directly, and individual investor yields will differ based on their actual holdings. Investing in stock is subject to fluctuation and possible loss of principal, whereas bonds, if held to maturity, offer a guarantee of principal.

So why is it that our society seems to believe stocks are fraught with risk when, historically, that doesn't seem to hold true?

Returning to something I discussed earlier in the book about what happens around the dinner table, I think such fear is inherited. The terror of a stock market crash capable of wiping out a lifetime of savings is so ingrained that it brings back generational stories of the Great Depression in the 1930s. The Depression was indeed tragic, leaving generational scars. Retirees fear investing in the ownership of companies in the form of stocks, because those stocks can crash. No wonder less than 50 percent of our population has any investments in stocks.

Good investment behavior means paying attention to both the value of your investments *and* the income you receive from those investments in the form of dividends. Since 1960, the cash dividend of the S&P 500 has increased at a compound rate of 5.76 percent, versus about 3 percent for inflation or the CPI. Once income is required, people shouldn't spend their principal; they should spend the income from their principal. So why is there such an emphasis on the daily fluctuation of principal?

Ownership in American companies represents the direct ownership of the earnings, cash flow, dividends, and net assets of the very businesses you frequent each day. Ownership can be in the form of your 401(k), mutual funds, ETF products, or direct ownership in the actual shares of companies. Prices fluctuate on the stock market, but long-term values are driven by real earnings and real dividends.

Yet most people see stock prices as random and inherently unstable. These distractions keep people from understanding and focusing on what's important: *when you own shares of a company, you are an owner of that company.*

AN INDUSTRY BUILT ON SELLING DOUBT

Financial advisors typically follow three steps when onboarding a new client.

1. **First, define their goals.** Where do they want to go?
2. **Next comes a plan.** This is the recipe for working toward their goals with actionable and measurable steps.
3. **Then comes implementation, the enactment of the plan.**

The first two steps lay out the *what* of your financial future; the last deals with the *how*.

All too often, investors make it through the first steps with optimism and progress, only to be led astray with the last. This is when experts, products, advertisements, advisors, and everyone else in the financial world tell you their way is best. And all the others? Well, they just don't measure up.

Of course, this leaves investors with a problem. *Who can you trust?* The stakes aren't small. This is a life's savings for many. It's the money investors will rely on for their thirty to forty or more years of retirement. But with so much doubt and confusion, how can they choose who to trust?

This is a hard question. Trust is built over time. Like exercise, it takes repetition. As a financial advisor, I live by the principle: *do what you say you're going to do when you say you're going to do it, and always, always, act in the best interest of the client.* But relationships take time to foster. If you're looking for help, you may not already have a trustworthy relationship with someone in finance. In blank-slate instances like this, I think it helps to examine the agendas of everyone involved. With a clear understanding of their *whys*, it's easier to make an informed decision.

Who are the players on the financial scene? I think there are four big ones: *financial manufacturers, media, salespeople,* and *advisors.*

Financial manufacturers are companies that create mutual funds, bonds, or other investments. They monitor demand and develop products that people think they want. Their sales are generated by uncertainty in the marketplace. Want to switch stocks? They will sell them to you and profit from the transaction. Want to add some bonds? Again, they will sell those to you too. When your doubt leads to an action, they generate revenue. As a business, their agenda is *profit*—not *your financial future.*

So, if manufacturers profit from doubt, doesn't it benefit them to create more of it? **That's where *the media* comes into play.** In the media, a twenty-four-hour news cycle leads to a focus on the here and now. In this fast-paced environment, "talking heads" share their opinions and financial forecasts with almost zero accountability. These differing viewpoints generate doubt, questioning, and in the end, change. Consider the number of sponsored talk-radio shows, many of which are really thirty-minute financial commercials. These shows help fund the station's operations. Again, as a business, their agenda is profit—not your financial future.

Next, we have *financial salespeople* and *advisors*. After forty years in this industry, I've seen great salespeople and great advisors, but rarely are they the same person. How do you determine which is which? Ask yourself:

- **Does my advisor *solve a problem* or *sell me a product*?** Investments (products) in and of themselves don't create financial confidence, income growth, generational wealth, or a lasting legacy.
- **Is this person helping me *to transact* or are they helping me *to get where I want to go*?** Do they ask questions and listen? Do they really understand my goals, fears and risks, most significant opportunities, and strengths? If so, do they help me along the way?
- **Are they a fiduciary who puts my interests first— before the company they work for and their own personal interests?**
- **Who writes their paycheck?** If they work for a large broker-dealer company, you might consider where their loyalty lies: to you or the company.

Unfortunately, many advisors don't have complete freedom to

recommend what might actually be suitable for a client, putting the burden on you to decide if their recommendation is really in your best interest. And if that's the case, what's the benefit of working with that advisor in the first place? Avoid advisors whose interests may conflict with yours, and request absolute transparency regarding kickbacks an advisor may be receiving. All too often, the "advisors" you'll find are thinly veiled salesmen for their parent companies.

This was one of the driving forces behind my choice to be independent. Without a company pushing products on me, I can provide clients with advice that works for them. Our independence is a defining principle. Our clients are our only bosses, which means we have complete freedom to recommend an approach that fits our client, not the sales agenda of a behind-the-scenes company.

The goal is to find someone whose agenda aligns with your own. Retirement planning isn't a one-time project. It's an ongoing partnership with the goal of ensuring you have enough money, and for long enough, to find the freedoms you desire. It's a large endeavor and one that usually requires a team of people to help tackle the complexities, paperwork, and strategies needed to make it happen.

In choosing members of your investment team, examine their agendas to decide if the foundation of trust is there. Over time, let trust develop. If something doesn't seem right, get a second opinion. This work may seem monotonous, but it can make all the difference in your financial future.

PLANNING TO HANDLE THE UNCONTROLLABLE

Longevity, volatility, inflation, distraction, and doubt all work together to shake your foundation and encourage you to stray from your plan. There's no eliminating them, so investors must learn to understand and deal with these issues. The challenge is approaching these with a level head, free of emotion or opinion.

As an example, longevity simply doesn't matter if you have a meaningful plan and understand how that plan will help you throughout your life. If you don't harbor the fear of running out of money before your passing, you can learn to embrace all the time you're given. A well-thought-out plan helps give you the freedom to enjoy the extra time, not fear it.

We cannot control these elements, but we can learn how to make the emotions associated with them work for, rather than against, us. In doing so, I think you'll find not only more confidence in your portfolio and financial plan, but a better outlook on life.

CHAPTER 5

The Things We Can Control

As an investor, your objectives are twofold:

1. First, find investments that can help your wealth to grow over time, working toward the goal of a bigger future for yourself and your family.

2. Second, manage those investments in a way that continues working toward your goals, knowing (to quote Kenny Rogers again) when to *hold them and when to fold them.*

But therein lays the challenge: how do you know when that is? How do you know when it makes sense to change an investment, especially those that have grown well, or those whose future you believe in?

My greatest mistakes have almost always been errors in judgement on when to sell. I'm not talking about panic selling; I've never let doubt caused by a "correction" persuade me to sell something I didn't want to let go. No, instead my mistakes often involved selling a great company simply because it had done well—a concept I've talked a bit about in this book as a poor strategy or common mistake.

Popular tickers today serve as frequent reminders of these losses. I remember when I owned them, and when I decided to sell them—Charles Schwab, Amazon, Google, Zoom, Berkshire Hathaway, etc. I made a great return on my investment in these companies, but had I simply sat on them...well, you know the rest.

Looking back, it's tough to reflect on my decision-making at the time. What led to my decision to sell these companies? I don't recall needing the cash immediately for something like a large purchase. Rather, it was simply the belief that they had performed really well. *How long could they continue in this way?*

Therein is the switch from a logical perspective to an emotional one. Logically, they could continue to perform well, and they did!

Strong companies tend to be strong for a reason. But I let my emotions get the better of me. Ultimately, I couldn't control how these companies performed, nor could I control their stock prices. But I could have better controlled my emotional response.

This becomes your ultimate job as an investor: managing your behavior is every bit as important as managing what is and isn't in your portfolio. When to buy, when to sell...these are all decisions to be made, and the more you can make them devoid of emotion, the better off you might be.

With that in mind, let's explore some of the emotions that frequently arise when dealing with investments and what you can do to flex your emotional muscles to keep them in check.

EMOTIONS

FEAR

Shark Week is among the longest-running and most popular cable programs in history. First appearing thirty years ago in 1988, the show has since been watched and celebrated by millions. Why would a program about sharks and their danger be so popular? I think it's because it plays on the emotion of fear, and more interestingly, people's desire to be a little bit scared.

This is quite the paradox: some people enjoy engaging in an activity designed to make them uncomfortable. The same can be said for horror movies or roller coasters. In these circumstances, however, the fear is often wholly unfounded. Sharks are responsible for about six deaths per year, and I highly doubt zombies will be taking over the world anytime soon. Nor do most roller coasters result in death or dismemberment. Instead, people should be much more afraid of mosquitos, with their death toll last year of more than 1,000,000 people (AMCA 2021).

My point is this: sometimes our greatest fears are the most unfounded. Whether it's an oversized fish or monsters under the bed, our worst fears take up a large portion of our conscious and drive actions that can be damaging and counterproductive. Fear is a powerful emotion, and one you must learn to rein in if you want to be a better investor.

There are many models to describe what sorts of things people fear—along with what motivates them to act. Behavioral psychologists will tell you that people are driven to run from pain and toward reward. People will run faster from a burning building than they will toward a chocolate cake. Only one represents certain, imminent danger.

But not all dangers bring the threat of life or limb. *Self-determination theory* suggests we're motivated by things that contribute to *our autonomy, relatedness, and certainty* (Ryan and Deci 2000). When we feel a threat in one of these areas, our response may still be fear. This, in turn, may cause us to react in one of three standard ways: fight, flee, or freeze.

How does this play out when investing? Financial losses, whether real or perceived, may trigger humans' bigger fears—launching behaviors that may not suit our portfolio. A dip in our stocks' value could trigger fears of losing autonomy to live independently, relate with our peers, or face a certain future.

As we've discussed, psychological studies suggest that for investors, a loss is twice as mentally powerful as a similar gain. The emotional pain of losing $20 would require a $40 gain to offset. That's a big problem when investors pay constant attention to their full portfolios and the swings happening at any given time.

If there's one thing that's important to understand: *volatility does not create risk; risk creates volatility.* We must remain resilient in the face of our own emotions and understand this fact.

JP Morgan puts out an insightful document once per quarter called "Guide to the Markets." In this document is a chart that shows two simple things: the lowest the market got during the year, and the point at which it finished the year. Most years see some level of decline at their worst, many even into the double digits, only to finish the year up double digits. In other words, markets will wiggle, but historically they go up more often than they go down. That has always been true; see graphic for details (J.P. Morgan 2021).

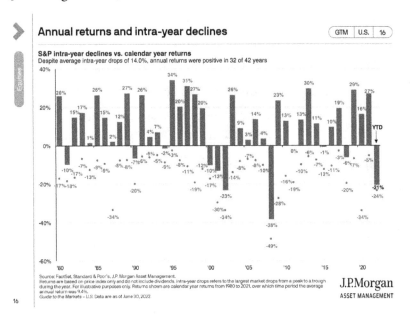

Annual returns and intra-year declines GTM U.S. 16

S&P intra-year declines vs. calendar year returns
Despite average intra-year drops of 14.0%, annual returns were positive in 32 of 42 years

Source: FactSet, Standard & Poor's, J.P. Morgan Asset Management.
Returns are based on price index only and do not include dividends. Intra-year drops refers to the largest market drops from a peak to a trough during the year. For illustrative purposes only. Returns shown are calendar year returns from 1980 to 2021, over which time period the average annual return was 9.4%.
Guide to the Markets – U.S. Data are as of June 30, 2022.

J.P.Morgan
ASSET MANAGEMENT

16

Investing isn't for a day, week, or even year. We measure investment returns over long periods of time. So why not use the same timeframe for measuring volatility? If we did, measuring volatility on scales of decades would make most troubling (and "scary") events look almost non-existent.

When bad news comes along, it feeds fear. Fear leads to withdrawals (fleeing), and withdrawals lead to the volatility we see as investors. Stock market wiggles don't create increased risk. Rather it's the investors jumping in and out—the ones allowing their emotions to get the better of them—that are at the root of increased risks.

The wiggles represent fear, but they shouldn't cause fear. But all too often, they do. We recently were interviewing a prospective client who said he was "nearly destroyed" in the 2008–2009 market decline, which caused him to move his investments out of the stock market and into less volatile certificates of deposits (CDs). Now that the market has rebounded, he was considering a move back into the market, preferably with an aggressive strategy.

This is someone who let the wiggles dictate his investment strategy. He allowed fear to get the best of him, and he sat on the sidelines for one of the greatest bull markets we've ever seen. Now, just as the market is entering what many financial professionals consider to be the later innings of the ballgame, this client wants to get aggressive.

The ghosts of 1929 and 2008 are burned deeply into the minds of many people. This fear is perpetuated with what feels like a never-ending stream of bad news—political unrest, pandemics, and whatever's around the corner. It's interesting how financial pundits may appear to be "smart" when they are cautious or nervous about what might happen, what might go wrong, and how uncertain the future might be. If you use historical facts to judge their advice, however, you quickly realize the "smart," overly cautious perspective has been, more often than not, incorrect.

Let's face it, everything in the future is uncertain. My career includes five large, fear-driven market "crises" that come to mind: Black Monday in 1987, Y2K in 1999, the World Trade Center attacks in 2001, the recession in 2008, and the onset of the COVID-19 pandemic in early 2020. Though these events are all unique, they were all the same in many ways.

With the perspective time has provided, we can say these events:

- Led to or were created by a fear of the unknown.
- Were impactful in many ways not immediately apparent at the time.
- Were seemingly an end to "the way it's always been."
- Were going to endanger the "American way of life."

While none of these outcomes ultimately came to fruition, these events did represent a significant buying opportunity for long-term investors. Each of these events altered the course and landscape of our country. We lost lives, jobs, savings, and sleep. Yet our country has always performed best when the chips were down. That's when we pull together to do what's necessary, and it can be an excellent opportunity to purchase assets from those overcome by fear.

Fear is a difficult emotion to tame. It goes against our innate nature of fight, flight, or freeze. **Deep down in our subconscious is a warning bell developed over thousands of years designed to keep us alive and out of harm's way.** Combined with the herd mentality, "my neighbor is stocking up on toilet paper, so maybe I should too," we get situations quickly spiraling out of control. Consider how this applies to each of the events just mentioned.

- **October 19, 1987, saw a decline of about 23 percent in the Dow Jones, the largest single-day percentage drop in the history of the market.** The cause? Investors utilizing computers designed to provide "portfolio insurance" that, when triggered by a decline, would sell assets. The computers took over, selling begets selling, and what do you have at the end of the day? A mess. Only when someone unplugged the computers and human judgment and reason took hold did things calm down. Three months later, the market was back in positive territory.

- **The last quarter of 1999 had people in a frenzy.** Convinced the computers we all relied on for everything from piloting aircraft to monitoring our library checkouts wouldn't be able to reconcile the rollover of their internal calendars from 99 to 00 at midnight, people started to panic. They filled bathtubs with water, sold all their stock, and returned their library books lest they owe 100 years of late fees.

- **The attacks on 9/11 had a much more significant impact on our country than the previous examples.** The outcome was more serious, and the effects more lasting. We're reminded of this lingering fear every time we step into an airport and pass through TSA screening. Immediately following the attacks, few wanted to travel for fear of another attack. The market closed for an entire week.

- **From 2008–2009, the market indices saw a broad decline of about 57 percent, thanks to a financial system that was overleveraged, overbought (mostly real estate), and entirely over its skis.** The fear was that the system itself wouldn't survive, that the rottenness had embedded itself so profoundly, there would be no way out. Yet liquidity returned to the markets, and they began to function again. From March 2009 until February 2020, the S&P 500 delivered an annualized rate of return of 16.7 percent. On February 19, 2021, the index stood some five times higher than the March 2009 temporary trough—in just eleven years.

- **Then came COVID-19, which felt very different.** The speed at which everything happened felt surreal, with the market losing about a third of its value in a little over a month. The change in employment from record lows to record highs was and still is staggering. The response from both the government and Federal Reserve was so massive, it is difficult to comprehend.

But the more things change, the more they stay the same.

People were afraid, and perhaps rightly so. But as investors, we cannot let fear drive our investment decisions. There's a reason most elevators aren't made of glass. If they were, people would be terrified to watch as they're buzzed up and down floors. Instead, our nature prefers to get in, push a button, and just be told when we're at our level. We don't need to see it happen; heck, we don't want to see it happen. All we want is to know the system works, and that we'll make it to the twenty-third floor without having to climb all those stairs—or risk plummeting to our death.

In March 2020, the market declined 12.5 percent. In April, it rose 12.6 percent. Twelve stories down and then back up would be very stressful if we saw the elevator working. But all we need to know is we landed up one floor.

Our financial system works. It always has. Sure, it's broken down a time or two, but America is the best repair company in the world. COVID-19 will eventually join those "black swan events" about which people write financial Armageddon books (and by the time you read this, perhaps you will already know how the next chapter turns out). This isn't a prediction nor a statement of fact, but rather an observation of human nature and behavior. We seem to have these periodic, unpredictable, unknown times when we're rattled temporarily, then march higher to new levels of productivity, progress, and accomplishment.

Learning to conquer your fears is an endeavor many spend their entire lives pursuing. While few will come face-to-face with a shark, almost all of us will need to stare down a bear market—and all the emotions that come with it—at some point. When the time comes, guard your portfolio and your feelings. Whether you're feeling hesitation, fear, or even anticipation and excitement, recognize that these are emotional reactions, not logical ones. Fall back on your game plan and use it to land where you want to be.

FOMO

When you're stuck in traffic on the interstate, creeping along, do you find yourself wanting to switch from one lane to another? Do you glance to the left, see the "fast lane" and become envious of how quickly they are moving? You look for an opening, signal, and move over to gain some speed...only to come to a stop. You then notice the car you were following in the lane to the right moves past you. A few minutes later, it has moved way ahead, out of sight.

This is an illustration to which investors can relate. Making a move from one strategy to another—one that looks more attractive because it is moving along faster than you—often has the same frustrating result. As with driving, you may take the risk and make a financial strategy change to feel like you're getting ahead, only to find yourself coming to a stop. You made that investment at the wrong time or for the wrong reason. This is FOMO or the Fear of Missing Out.

Buying an investment in today's world is rather easy. From apps on your phone to mutual fund stores in strip malls, purchasing investments has never been simpler. What previously involved a call to your broker to make an investment purchase is now even easier with these multiple alternatives. Investment companies, however, thrive on investors making changes, whether it comes from transaction commissions or asset management fees.

Some financial companies encourage lane-changing behavior, where investors hop from one product or strategy to another, in an attempt to "beat the market." Frankly, beating the market requires a lot of work (and luck). You must buy something before the value rises, sell it high, and reinvest those dollars in the next low-value stock that goes up in price. One's ability to do this consistently is practically non-existent. The bottom line is that investing takes discipline. Yet people believe they can, spurred on by a variety of messaging they receive.

We also know that FOMO has a close cousin: *comparison*. It seems only natural for people to compare. Comparing is said to be human nature. We tend to examine what we have and make, how we look, and where we live—comparing it to that of our neighbor, friend, colleague, celebrity, or anyone else we bring into our consciousness.

The funny thing about this habit is that there's never a winner.

That's because there will always be someone somewhere with more than you have, who looks better than you do, who has a bigger house, etc. Comparing your progress to your neighbor's, to those on social media, or even to your own idea of where you "should" be is a recipe for trouble. Comparing yourself to someone else, or to an ideal, only generates negative feelings and emotions. **The habit of comparison envelops people and can significantly harm their investment behavior.** It plants the seed for FOMO and leads to comparing how fast you're going versus the person in the other lane.

The only healthy comparison to make is your current situation with your past. It is a comparison that hopefully demonstrates progress. Comparing your progress with an ideal creates anxiety, frustration, feelings of doubt, and even hopelessness. Measuring your progress looking back creates feelings of confidence, accomplishment, and happiness.

I encourage my clients to measure progress. *Are you on plan or target? If so, great! If not, what adjustments do you need to make to get back in your lane and move toward your destination?* Measuring how far you've come is much healthier than judging against perfection. Measure progress, not perfection.

At the end of the day, the only reason people invest and save is for income—either for today or tomorrow. Attempting to grow your money pile bigger and bigger may sound appealing, but there are times when the money pile may shrink instead of grow. When that time comes, pulling income out will hit twice as hard. Not only are you selling when prices are down, but you have to sell more to hit your necessary income amount. Trying to trade your way up the pile is a lot of work, and a goal for which few have the skill and discipline to achieve.

On the contrary, stay focused on a strategy with a quality track record. Ignore the whispering emotions of fear or greed, and you can reach your destination with a lot less "lane-changing risk." Decide your destination and map out a course. Be very careful making those lane changes.

REGRET

Regret may be the most enduring and damaging emotion investors grapple with during their financial lives. As financial advisors, we see it from both sides: clients either regret having done something, or regret not having done something—or, more often, both. Like a cancer, regret can crawl into all facets of your financial life and encourage you to make bad decisions. All too often, it's successful.

What is regret? The way I see it, regret is the re-visitation of past mistakes. Maybe someone hit the panic button as the market dropped, only to watch investments rebound in a short period. Perhaps they jumped out at a good time but couldn't decide on a "right time" to jump back in, missing out on would-be gains. Investors watch themselves do this over and over, each time saying they "won't do it again." Then, when they inevitably do, the regret only deepens.

This vicious cycle can pour over into other areas of life. How often have we heard the stories of someone betting their life's savings just to have the outcome bounce the other way?

One such family was chronicled in the *Wall Street Journal* in May 2010. The Potyk family liquidated their investment portfolio to avoid the volatility they'd been experiencing. The article listed all the problems with the economy and markets and mentioned investors were abandoning stocks. Investors felt this was the smart thing to do, the article continued, as they thought the markets would be fundamentally different going forward (Browning 2010).

I don't know what happened to the Potyks. The *Journal* never wrote a follow-up to revisit their story. But I wonder how many years the family sat on the sidelines, distrustful of what would become one of the longest bull markets in US history. And if they did, do they now struggle with the regret of their decision? I imagine they must. This is just one of a thousand stories with similar patterns: emotional reactions to uncontrollable circumstances.

So how can we combat regret? What can we do to learn from past experiences without dwelling on the "woulda-coulda-shouldas?"

If regret is a child, its parents are fear and greed. When markets fall, the fear of loss rears its head. When prices rise, greed and envy of those who are "getting rich" may lead to the fear of missing out. Ultimately greed is just another form of fear. Giving in to either of these emotions often creates regret.

In short, regret is commonly caused by emotional reactions to uncontrollable events. Though we cannot control the uncontrollable (like what the market does on any given day), we can manage our reactions. We do this by creating a plan based on a foundation of logic, not emotion. Personal finance is more personal than it is finance, as I've mentioned—so we must try to account for feelings. For example, plans should be designed to encourage people to feel confident and strive to help them achieve the growth they seek. They are regular reminders in periods of uncertainty and fear. They prevent regret by tackling it at its source. Think about it: when was the last time you heard someone regret sticking to a plan?

I think gratitude is also a potent antidote to regret. It's easy to question past mistakes and wonder what could have been done differently. All the questions make it easy to lose sight of the answer you chose and the outcomes of the decisions you made. Ultimately, they all led you to where you are now. Isn't that something for which to be thankful? Something from which to learn? Searching for the gratitude hidden under layers of regret has had a profound effect on me and has led me to learn lessons from each mistake I've made.

If you play golf, you're probably familiar with the idea that you shouldn't let your past shots influence your next one. And if you play, you probably know how hard this is to do, especially if your previous shot sent you looking for your ball deep in the weeds of an adjacent hole. But hey, as a golfer would say, a bad day playing golf beats a good day working. **Make a plan, envision the outcome, and take the shot. Make the next shot a good one, and watch the joy of your progress erase the pain of regret.**

PERSPECTIVE

OPTIMISM IS A REQUIREMENT

Following national headlines would have you believe we're moments away from catastrophe, teetering on the edge of sheer doom. It's an easy narrative in which to engage, especially when we hear it every minute of every day. The problem is that repetition often convinces people, and once convinced, people tend to ignore logic. That pessimism is poisonous for investors.

Now I'm not going to tell you that everything in our world is great, but the reality is things are pretty good. I could argue that our world is better than it has ever been.

When you think about it, being an investor requires a positive mindset. It necessitates the belief that the future will be better. After all, the reason you're willing to take some of your hard-earned cash and invest it in something means you're optimistic about the prospects of that something. Combine this belief with the patience required to be a long-term investor, and the investment tends to pay off.

On a long enough time horizon, patience has always paid off. The market is far higher today than it was twenty, fifty, or one hundred years ago.

Over long time periods, things are unquestionably getting better. According to Our World in Data, across six significant areas of health and social progress, our world has improved by leaps and bounds (Roser 2020). As a society, we're healthier, wealthier, and smarter than we have ever been. So what's up with all the negativity?

Ask yourself this: how has literacy changed over the past day, week, and month? Frankly, the "good" in society is much more difficult to measure over a short time than the "bad." When bad things happen, they usually unfold quickly—and energy and time are spent quantifying them. This makes them newsworthy, which is how they end up in your ear, day in and day out. A tragedy is more apt to make breaking news than a kind act. This constant negativity makes it easy to extrapolate and assume, which are two more behaviors we're continually fighting.

This negativity leads to extrapolation. "All I hear is bad news; the world must be falling apart." But extrapolation without data is an assumption, and assumptions are often false.

The book, *Factfulness*, by Hans Rosling, is an excellent read on how a *negative bias* creates instincts that shade our viewpoint. This, in turn, causes us to develop beliefs in our minds that defy historical facts, which in turn cause us to behave in ways that are not necessarily good for our future (Rosling et al. 2020).

The negative bias causes us to tune in more to bad news than good news. As a result, if we don't consciously work on it, we're more apt to dwell and act strongly on this bad news (Cherry 2020).

This disposition hits people hard, both in their portfolios and mental well-being. Pick a poll, and the conclusion is the same: *despite progress in so many areas, people in America are generally "less happy" than they have been.* There are many strategies on how to improve happiness or manage your interpretation of negative news, but I won't explore those here. Remember, however, it is essential to recognize the effect this may have on your decision-making and therefore your finances.

The best thing investors can do is look at the future from a balanced, positive viewpoint. Having an optimistic view is the only realism. It's the only worldview in line with the historical record.

All you need to do is look around and consider how much better we are today, even though nostalgia is one heck of a drug. We believe things will continue to get better—that's what happens when you have free markets and incentives to create value and success for others. It is a remarkable system.

To remain optimistic as an investor, understand that focusing on your portfolio isn't necessarily healthy. There will always be something wrong with a company on any given day.

Yet every crisis can create opportunity. Who doesn't like that? Take the long view. This is how companies manage their businesses. They don't make daily changes in their direction, initiatives, or products. So why should you? Financial providers make activity or transactions far too easy, allowing you to jump in and out of investments, transforming people from investors to speculators.

Turn off the noise. Headlines sensationalize nearly everything, even the weather. And while that sometimes may be an accurate assessment, it often produces unnecessary fear. It also only represents one slice of time and one point on the planet.

In general, what happens moment by moment, every day, is more random than real. The media must continuously provide a narrative to explain the randomness. Before you know it, the noise reprograms you from being an investor to a short-term speculator. You are motivated to react, which often means advertisers win, and you lose.

Being persistently optimistic about the future keeps you *invested and on track toward your goals.* As investors, that's what we're after.

ADOPT A PROSPERITY MINDSET

Wealth is a mindset. In my years as a financial advisor, I've worked with many wealthy individuals who have everyday-type jobs. From bus drivers to teachers, entrepreneurs to an administrative assistant at the Chamber of Commerce, I've learned that income isn't the best determinate of future wealth. Instead, it's a mindset, one I like to call the *prosperity mindset.*

A prosperity mindset looks at the whole equation: your daily spending, saving for your future, and yes, even how much you make. But more importantly, it focuses on what you choose to do with your money, not necessarily your ability to acquire more of it.

There are three ideologies wrapped up in a prosperity mindset:

1. **First, *take a long-term approach.*** A better way to overcome the day-to-day fearmongering is to take a long approach. Building wealth doesn't happen overnight. Force it, and you risk wrecking a portfolio.

2. **Second, *avoid emotional decisions.*** Before making any decisions, big or small, I like to take a moment, check in with myself, and ask: *What's going on today? Is the decision I'm about to make a good one? Are there things going on right now that could muddy my decision-making ability? Is this a good time to make this choice?* These questions help me understand whether emotion or logic is driving my decision.

3. **If the decision is one of sound mind and logic, the third criterion is to *determine if it's an informed choice.*** Ask yourself: *Have I thought through this option? If I'm uncomfortable, have I consulted other experts to gather their thoughts?* In finance, this might translate to diversification, portfolio allocation, and risk exposure.

Together, these mental exercises help drive a prosperity mindset. Let's look at how they apply to finance specifically.

I mentioned that income isn't a great way to determine if someone will be wealthy. Think about it like this: If I make $50,000 and spend $40,000, I have $10,000 left over to save. If I make $1 million and spend $1.2 million, I'm $200,000 in the hole.

The person who saves $10,000 is far wealthier than the high earner. Therefore, what you choose to do with your money is far more important than how much of it you make. It's a mental hurdle, and not without its caveats or exceptions. But regardless of any other criteria, a disposition to spend less than you make is a vital tenant of a prosperity mindset.

Now take that savings amount and apply a long-term approach. Consider an example of two workers, Ellen Early and Larry Later, who happen to be the same age. Ellen starts saving $2,000 per year at age twenty-five and stops at thirty-five, which equates to total savings over ten years of $20,000. Her friend Larry starts saving $2,000 per year from age thirty-five to sixty-five, saving three times as much, a total of $60,000 saved. Assume they earn the same rate of return of 8 percent per year. At sixty-five, Ellen has $291,546, and Larry has $256,566. **The lesson: start early and save consistently throughout your career.**

Think about your finances in seven or eight goals. These could be things like saving 15 percent of your income, or "making work a choice" at sixty-two instead of sixty-five. Describe the best and worst outcomes for each of those goals. Think about what you can do to start making progress toward those goals and what is within your power to control.

The market will wiggle, but it can't change the choices you make for yourself. These you have complete control over. If you want the ability to make choices about what you do with your time, your interests, and your relationships, start now. The real reason for saving and accumulating wealth is freedom. And freedom, like prosperity, is a mindset.

THE SMART WAY TO MEASURE YOUR WEALTH

How do you measure your wealth? Most people assume there are two typical ways. The first is a simple money calculation that takes everything you own, subtracts everything you owe, and that formula gives you your net worth. Simple. Others say wealth isn't a measure of the money one has but of the intangibles such as relationships, time, health, etc.

The trouble with the first approach is that money is simply a scorecard, a measure of available resources quantified in dollar bills. It misses out on everything that the second approach captures: the wealth found in personal connection and freedom of time. But it's hard to pay your bills with friendship, so the second method misses out on some of the pragmatism found in the first.

As a result, I think it's essential to measure wealth with a combination of the two and with one simple word: value.

Money is a byproduct of creating value for others. We are

paid for the value we provide to others, and we pay others for the value they create for us. For example, I have no idea how the water in my plumbing works, but I know that in exchange for a number of dollars, I can hire someone who has spent their life understanding how it works and what's needed to keep it working. They create value for me with their skillset.

Likewise, I create value by helping others understand what's important about money and guiding them toward a bigger future. I receive money in exchange for that value.

So really, our wealth isn't in the money we have, but rather in our ability to make that money. Our wealth doesn't come from the dollars themselves but from the knowledge and skills that generate those dollars. That's our value, and that's where we find the confidence so many are seeking.

In *Total Cash Confidence*™, author Dan Sullivan refers to the acronym K.A.S.H. or knowledge, attitude, skills, and habit. Taken together, these attributes are what create confidence. K.A.S.H. confidence comes from understanding that you can provide value to someone when they want something done but don't want, or know how, to do it.

Going one step further, I think our wealth is a function of our value. Creating value for others often results in payment for that value. Create more value, receive more money. This recurring loop creates an endless marketplace of wealth for those who can help others.

That payment may be monetary, but it also applies to relationships. Think about it: we invest our time and energy in those we choose to have around us. We create value by being there when they need us and receiving value when they do the same. In this way, our measure of wealth captures both the tangible and intangible. Whether the deposits go into our emotional bank or our regular bank, we can improve our wealth through the value we create.

This is why so many people struggle with the traditional idea of retirement. When people strive to achieve a certain portfolio balance and then quit their career, they aren't retiring to anything. They aren't *going to something*; they *are moving away.*

When people are in the creation phase, their futures are more extensive. They receive intellectual, emotional, and resource deposits. When they "arrive" at a number or an age and then decide to quit creating value and retire, their future tends to shrink. If the value of their portfolio decreases when they're no longer creating value for others, fear often sets in.

Having worked with many traditionally "wealthy" people who created their wealth by working, saving, and investing, I can tell you that few derive confidence from the value of their portfolios. Regardless of how much they may have, they're happy when stock prices are up and sad when prices are down (especially if someone they know is up while they're down). If prices are up, they're nervous about when prices will drop. The handwringing never stops.

True wealth is about helping others to have a bigger and better future. Everything about your future is about your knowledge, attitude, skills, and habits and the confidence created by using them to create value for others. You no longer have tension about money; instead, you're confident because you can produce it again by creating value and receiving payment. This formula keeps you permanently ahead and in a mentality of abundance. It's value creation, and it tends to magnetize you to people with similar outlooks on life.

Creating and improving value for others is stimulating. This perspective endeavors to build a bigger future for yourself and those around you. In my mind, that's the true measure of a person's wealth.

BUILDING GOOD HABITS

AVOID GETTING BOGGED DOWN

The average American spends more than eighty-five hours per month watching TV. The same person will likely spend about 272 hours sleeping and 158 hours working. Know how much time they'll spend working on their finances? About 1.8 minutes per day, or a little less than one hour per month (Arends 2019).

It seems crazy to me that people will spend an hour on Yelp trying to find the perfect taco bar for dinner but will invest thousands of dollars based on a thirty-second spot on the *Mad Money* TV show. For many households, more time is spent planning a vacation than planning retirement. Vacations last a week or two, but a thirty-year retirement lasts 1,560 weeks.

I understand that you may find finance boring, and for many Americans, the picture can be bleak (or even downright depressing). Put those sentiments together, and you get a recipe for procrastination and avoidance.

That's a potent combination. These individuals have no idea how much they spend, what they spend it on, how much (or how little) they save, or how their finances are working in their lives. They may live paycheck-to-paycheck and either hope to "figure things out later" or throw their hands in the air in disgust over their situation.

On the other hand, I've seen people who spend too much time on their finances. They obsess over every minor detail. They love to debate the minutia on every money matter, most of which are entirely out of their control. They worry about how the government is out to take advantage of them or which geopolitical events will bring down the entire financial system. They focus on small things, like clipping coupons or finding the gas station that will save them two cents a gallon, but don't have a grasp on the big picture items that matter.

One person is so overwhelmed that they never get started. The other is so bogged down with details that they can't see the forest through the trees. Both get to the same place financially—nowhere.

The reality is that nobody really gets educated about money. It is rarely taught in schools, and is often introduced as an afterthought in some professional curriculums. Most people learn by doing or making mistakes as they go. For something as important as finance, this is a terrifying prospect. Just ask any of those with outrageous student loans. Can you imagine if we educated surgeons or engineers this way with their professions? Finance may not bring life or death, but it certainly can bring freedom or servitude.

Life is busy. The goal isn't for you to spend more of your time on your finances. Actually, the opposite is true. Do things that give you emotional, intellectual, and resource deposits, not just financial ones.

Ignoring your finances and praying for a financial windfall isn't an option, nor is micromanaging your personal finances every single day. Eventually, you'll either lose your mind, drive your friends and family crazy, or mess things up by overthinking and overreacting.

Activity is easy, but also dangerous. Just look at all the selling by financial companies. They want you to trade. But spending more time on your portfolio doesn't guarantee success.

Mr. Buffett is right: too much thought and activity around your portfolio can be detrimental to your investment performance. He's famous for suggesting people limit their investment decisions to twenty "slots" *during their lifetime.* It makes you very intentional and careful about your choices and decisions (Kaplan 2017).

So what do we suggest? Take the time to set up a financial plan. Sketch out a potential roadmap and think about where you want to go. Building a plan takes time upfront, but working the plan can be done with a minimal time investment. Take a couple of hours and work through these five things:

1. **Income and career choice.** This is your most important investment. Is it working for you?
2. **Spending rate.** People like this word better than "budget." Where is your money going?
3. **Savings rate.** Start early and save till it hurts. Let time and compounding work for you.
4. **Housing.** This is typically your most significant monthly expense. We're fans of paying it off as quickly as possible. A debt-free lifestyle is a happy lifestyle with more freedom and options.
5. **Transportation.** This is necessary and expensive. Cars lose value, so limit the resources you put into them.

Have a plan that reflects your goals. Have a system and monitor your progress. Use an accountability buddy if that helps. Find someone you trust to advise you when the inevitable uncertainties arise in life. Pay attention to these five areas, and you'll be ahead of most Americans.

From there, managing your finances every month is much easier. We suggest automating as much as possible:

- Automate your bills to avoid late fees and dings on your credit report.
- Automate your savings to various accounts (retirement, 529, HSAs, travel, emergencies, etc.).
- Make sure your emergency account stays topped off with three to six months of your spending rate.
- Use a separate project account to save for large, expected purchases (remodels, Christmas gifts, new car, vacations, etc.).
- Track your spending using any of the available apps (but choose wisely, as developers will be able to see your spending and market to you), or use old-school methods like reviewing your bank statements or credit card reports.
- Review your progress annually. Have an accountability partner or an advisor who works for you.

Managing your money is nowhere near as exciting as *Game of Thrones*. But if you take the time to think it through and build a plan, you'll still have time to catch up on the latest episodes and one day be able to make work a choice.

Improving investor behavior starts not with *investments*, but with *investors*. That's you. Build a plan, work the plan, and review it once a year. It can pay dividends for you in the years to come.

UNDERSTAND HOW INTEREST WORKS FOR YOU

Anyone who has ever spent time outdoors understands and appreciates the value of a sharp knife. Whether stripping wood to start a fire, using it as a cooking utensil, cleaning a fish, or for any of a million other purposes, the trusty knife is an essential tool.

But knives also have inherent danger. Used the wrong way, a knife can quickly end a fun camping trip, or worse—a life.

With this in mind, let's consider *compound interest.* For those who don't understand the concept, **compound interest is money earned on money spent or saved, typically expressed as a percentage.** If you have a savings account, you've earned interest (albeit a tiny amount). **This interest is compounded (i.e., multiplied) when the amount is left alone over a period of time.**

For example, if you have $100 that earns 5 percent per year, you'll have $105 after the first year. If left alone, that $105 will be worth $110.25 the following year, not just the $110.00. Often referred to as the eighth wonder of the world, this compound interest is what drives investments and savings, and ultimately what allows people to retire.

Three essentials drive it:

1. **The amount saved** (the principal),
2. **The amount it earns** (interest rate expressed as a percentage), and
3. **Time** (how long is it allowed to work).

As investors, we seek to understand and control compound

interest. Like the knife, when used correctly, compound interest is a powerful tool. Even better, the three variables behind compound interest can be put to work for anyone, regardless of income or amount saved.

That's why we're big fans of starting early with savings. It puts time on your side. It's the single most significant variable of the three.

As we've discussed, time in the market will always beat timing the market. For example, let's say you had $10,000 to invest. If you could have invested in the S&P 500 at these decades, in December 2021 you would have:

- $46,036 if you had invested in 2010
- $46,202 if you had invested in 2000
- $240,288 if you had invested in 1990
- $1,104,989 if you had invested in 1980
- $2,048,669 if you had invested in 1970
- $4,392,394 if you had invested in 1960

This, of course, doesn't take into consideration fees, taxes, or other expenses. But it illustrates that investing in broad markets like those represented by S&P 500 over the long haul is an unmatched money-compounding machine.[1]

The key is *time*. The longer you are invested, the higher the probability of a good outcome. Investing long-term in a portfolio of great companies that sell their goods and services to everyone, every day, everywhere is what I describe as a *compounding financial*

---

[1] These figures were calculated for individual decades (Political Calculations 2006).

machine. Long-term ownership with this perspective helps protect the purchasing power of money—the goal of most investors.

UNDERSTAND HOW INTEREST WORKS AGAINST YOU

But like the knife, compound interest can wound or even kill if misused. **We've talked about how compound interest works with investments, but the same principles apply to debt.**

Unless you're the United States Federal Reserve, money cannot be printed out of thin air. Whenever you spend more money than you have, you must borrow money to fund that purchase.

On the other side of the deal is someone loaning you the money you need. Borrowing the money comes with a cost, one that benefits the person loaning you the money.

Again, **the three variables behind compound interest become essential:**

- How much you borrow,
- What your loan interest rate is, and
- The amount of time you will take to pay back the loan.

These can all have a dramatic impact on the amount you will ultimately pay.

For example, let's say you intend to purchase a $30,000 vehicle at 3 percent, with a plan to pay it off in six years. Your monthly payment would be about $456, which seems pretty average. But after six years, you will have paid about $2,818 in interest or almost an additional 10 percent of the original cost of the car.

Now $2,800 may not seem like a big deal, but apply the same math to other everyday expenses. A house purchased for $300,000 at 4 percent with a thirty-year mortgage has a monthly payment of about $1,432 (excluding additional costs like PMI, insurance, taxes, etc.). After thirty years of on-time payments, you will have paid an additional $215,608 in interest alone, meaning that a $300,000 home actually costs you $515,000.

Credit cards are even worse, thanks to their convenience and varying rates. According to creditcards.com, the average interest rate for a new credit card as of 2021 is a whopping 26 percent. Assuming you have a balance of $10,000 and you're paying the minimum every month (about $317), it will take you almost thirty years to pay off the debt, and you'll pay nearly $31,000 in total on a $10,000 balance!

If you bump that payment up to $500 per month, you'll pay off the amount in just over two years, paying a total of about $13,250. That's the power of compounding. An extra $183 per month saves you twenty-seven years of payments and about $18,000. If that's not enough reason to try and save a little extra each month, I don't know what is.

The lesson here is simple: compound interest is an extremely powerful tool, one with which too many are hurting themselves. What may seem like small steps at the beginning, like saving a couple of dollars here or making an extra payment there, can have a profound impact in the long term.

We may not be able to control the rate at which money will compound, but we can control the other two variables: the amount saved and the time invested. Make compound interest work for you. Those who genuinely understand compound interest earn it and never pay it.

MIND YOUR OWNED BUSINESSES

Another aspect that you can control as an investor is what businesses you invest in as a partial owner.

Most business owners can feel the pulse of their businesses. If you own a coffee shop, for instance, you can go to the location, see and interact with your employees, touch your inventory, and keep your customers happily caffeinated. You can smell the aroma of your business. You can feel it.

What if you had that same feeling as a shareholder of a public company? What if you thought like an owner? Consider one that sells coffee. Yesterday, you didn't own any shares of this company, but today you are an owner—a shareholder.

The feeling of being an owner of that company, however, often is divorced from the actual owning of a percentage or shares in a public company. Some may think those shares instead represent a lotto ticket that fluctuates every business day on some stock exchange, based on public consensus or what some analyst says or doesn't say about that company's prospects. Some almost consider it like a casino.

But when you think like an owner, your perspective changes.

Owning a share of that business can be an abstract thought. Owning your own coffee shop worth $1 million is just as valuable as owning $1 million worth of stock in that public company. You don't control the public company like you control your own business, but they have the same value to you. And if your genius is anything other than running a business daily, likely you are better off with passive equity ownership. Make no mistake, you are an owner of that business, albeit a minority owner, but still an owner! When you invest in shares of that company, you are not just buying numbers on a screen or in your account somewhere that goes up and down in price; you are buying real ownership in that business.

The beauty of the stock market is you can choose businesses in which you want to be part owner. Our whole investment philosophy is to *own great consumer companies that sell their goods and services to everyone, every day, everywhere.* Companies that can do that can make a profit, which can be shared with shareholders via a dividend. That's a tangible result of owning a part of the business. Dividends don't lie.

Being able to walk into a business of which you are an owner/shareholder offers a feeling of ownership one can't experience when owning shares of a mutual fund, exchange-traded fund, or any other financial product. And unlike running your own business, there's no day-to-day responsibility of opening the doors at 4:30 a.m., closing at 10:00 p.m., or managing payroll. Your only responsibility is to "open the envelope" each month when your investment statement arrives.

Good investor behavior also means you know, or can explain with two or three sentences, what you own. This is one of Buffett's fundamental principles. Peter Lynch once said, "Never invest in an idea you can't illustrate with a crayon." You don't need to make hundreds of successful investments over your savings and investing lifetime. Rather, invest in those companies that you know and can reasonably predict with a level of confidence that their products and services will be in demand, or that the management of the company will navigate for the benefit of the owners (you).

It has been said that the average time someone used to hold a share of stock back in the sixties was eight years. Now, it's claimed the average time is four months. We call this *renting your investments.* Buying and selling is akin to playing gin rummy with your investments, discarding and drawing from a deck of cards. Ideal owners make investments where the holding period is "forever."

CHOOSE GREAT COMPANIES TO OWN

But how do you choose in which companies to own a part? What makes one company more attractive than another? Most investors will attempt to discover what a company is "worth" to determine what price to pay for it, but that's more challenging than one would think.

What is Google worth? Most finance people would look up the share price, about $2,900, and multiply it by the number of shares to find what the company is currently "valued" at—about $1.9 trillion (as of January 31, 2022). But does value always equal precisely what a company is worth?

If Google were to go out of business tomorrow and have a fire sale—offering up everything they have from patents to buildings, desk chairs to web servers—the total output would be significantly less than $1.9 trillion. Likewise, if they were to announce a fully autonomous car, the value of the company could go up, likely by a significant amount.

The "worth" of a company goes beyond its present price to what the price could be in the future. Investors look at a company and say to themselves, "I like what they're doing, and I expect them to grow in the future," so they invest. They factor in a mix of intangibles—prospects for growth, risks, market conditions, and even a dash of hope—then decide to purchase a piece of that company. Collectively, these purchases form the current share price.

VALUING A BUSINESS OR INVESTMENT

I believe it is far more essential to evaluate your investments based on what we call the intrinsic value, a data-based evaluation of what we consider an investment to be worth rather than its current price. The current price is what I might be able to buy or sell the investment for at a given moment. It has nothing to do with the actual value of that investment.

Described another way, the current price of a company either overstates or understates the real value of that company at any given moment. Sometimes the price can swing dramatically, all while the company continues to do what it does every day—find value for its customers or clients. When the price gets too out of step with the value, it can create an opportunity (or a bubble).

We try to differentiate the *value of a company (worth)* versus the *price*. When you focus on the value of the company, your judgment is far more intelligent. You can determine whether to buy more because it's underpriced, hold it, or sell it because it's overpriced or the prospects for its future are no longer attractive. Price is simply what you could buy or sell at the moment.

Price is easy. We can look it up anytime and anywhere. The hard part is understanding the value of a company. There are many tools available that offer some insight: PE ratios, book values, and so forth. But there's more to it than that. It takes judgment, insight, research, and experience. Often, smart investments require a commitment to *go against the current pervasive view*. If a company is currently out of favor, it takes wisdom and experience to determine if the reasoning behind a sell-off is warranted or an overreaction.

Market prices are always in flux, which can be a significant distraction. So instead, we prefer to look at the fundamentals,

117

the operating results of companies, cash flow, earnings growth, and most important: dividends.

A track record of consistent dividends is a strong measure of a company's health. When they increase their dividends (which happens to be our focus), that exudes confidence that the leaders of the company have for the prospects of the company. Although the payment of dividends is not guaranteed, when paid out, dividends are always positive; price fluctuations *may* be positive or negative. Wise investors trust fundamentals more than the emotionally charged, day-to-day market or price behavior.

Many investors focus entirely too much time and attention on their account value rather than the income from their investments. They give little consideration to how well a company is doing and instead focus on the current price and news narrative.

Spending too much time attempting to predict what is going to happen, including both economically and politically, is often not a good use of your time and energy. Forecasts of economics and implications rarely turn out to be accurate; they are unpredictable and most often a waste of time. As Warren Buffet said in the 1994 *Annual Berkshire Hathaway* report, "We will continue to ignore political and economic forecasts which are an expensive distraction for many investors and businessmen" (Buffett 1995).

In summary, *mind your owned businesses.* Investors should seek to understand the value of their investments, not their current price. You can be a better investor if you check your actual dividend income *every ninety days* rather than checking your value *every ninety minutes.* It may not be as exciting as watching the daily fluctuation occurring on Wall Street, but bore me to death with rising dividend income, and I'll be a happy man.

THINK IN YEARS

There's $15 on the line, and your buddy is stepping up to a ten-footer for a birdie on the eighteenth hole. It's a slippery putt, but not slippery enough. As he takes his shot, human nature kicks in. "Miss it, miss it," we say to ourselves. But there's no level of hoping or wishing that will have any measurable effect on that putt.

As humans, we do this a lot. We look at all manner of situations and hope for different outcomes. We hope the Broncos win. We hope to live well into our hundreds. We hope the stock market goes up. In all these situations, there's very little we can do to affect what happens. We get so caught up hoping for one thing or another that we forget the little steps we can take to improve our odds of success. Living to one hundred is a hope; eating healthy and exercising is a choice. And when it comes to finance, choosing how much to save is far more important than hoping for better market returns.

Market performance tends to be the singular focus of investors and investment media alike. *How is the market performing? What are the benchmarks doing? At what level are my holdings?* All these questions are similar in one regard: they are reactionary. They focus on elements that can't be controlled.

Investment returns are important, as we've discussed. **The** magic of compounding interest, sometimes called the eighth wonder of the world, is what helps rigorous savers to retire as millionaires. But the amount you save can have a profound impact on the value of a portfolio over a lifetime. For compound interest to work its magic, it must have something on which to work. Consistency is a virtue, and it's an element you can control.

Life is filled with challenges, expenses, and emergencies, all of which can derail the best of intentions when it comes to saving. Having a method for saving becomes essential. Often that means "paying yourself first." For example, can you have your employer automatically contribute to your 401(k) from your paycheck? Great! The sting of savings might hurt at first, but after a couple of months, you may not notice it. That's the goal. We want to automate savings as much as possible. As a best practice, we encourage saving 10–25 percent of your income. The more you save, the better the outcome. It's better to save 10 percent every month than 25 percent once or twice a year. Save until it hurts and make it a habit.

Pensions once made this easy for would-be retirees. Employees didn't need to think about saving for retirement; it just happened. As retirement savings continue to shift away from companies and toward individual employees, making "saving" a routine becomes even more important. The great thing about independent alternatives such as 401(k) plans is they allow you to contribute at your savings rate. You get to control how much you want to put in and where that money is invested, as well as take comfort in knowing that it's your money, now and into the future. These plans are designed to reward diligent savers.

Tomorrow, the market may go up, down, or sideways. No one knows which way it will move, and those who say they do are just guessing. The problem with guessing is that it's inherently inconsistent. Some days you're right, and other days you're wrong. How much you choose to save is controlled only by you. The consistency with which you choose to save is a decision over which you have complete control. The more you save, the less the market must perform to end up with the same result. Steady saving over a lifetime helps take the "hoping" out of a retirement plan.

Praying to the golf gods won't help us win the round. What we can do is take lessons, get a coach, and practice. We can hit the driving range and improve our odds that by the last hole, it won't matter if our competitor sinks the ten-footer. Our goal is to stroll up to the eighteenth green a few shots ahead. This scenario relates to what consistent saving achieves. Make it a habit, practice it regularly, and watch your retirement account grow.

FOCUS ON THE IMPORTANT NUMBERS

Too many investors focus their attention on performance and prices. That is problematic for many reasons, but the biggest one is simple: you can't eat appreciating prices. Instead, we believe the most desirable outcome for investors is income. After all, that's what we use to buy food, make a car payment, or reinvest to grow further. Why do most people invest? Income. Whether you need that income today or tomorrow, most people invest with the belief that doing so will provide, maintain, or improve their income.

The problem is that some people tie their income directly to the performance of the market. After all, this is a common approach to investing.

1. Step one, buy a bunch of your desired asset class (stocks, bonds, gold, real estate).
2. Step two, hope their value improves over time.
3. Step three, sell the asset when the price has improved, using the proceeds for income.

But this is akin to a farmer selling off acres of his land. As the area shrinks, so does his ability to grow crops. It becomes a downward spiral, eventually leading to asset depletion. **This is what we refer to as a *growth for income* (emphasis on the "for") strategy, whereby growth is necessary "for" continued income.** Years like 2018 make this strategy hazardous. No growth means it's time for the farmer to sell some land, which makes generating income next year even more difficult.

The other risk is inflation. At a mere 3 percent inflation rate, the prices of food, fuel, and just plain living double every twenty-four years. That might seem like a long time, but that's the range of time between ages sixty and eighty-four. With better access to healthcare, science, and innovation—and taking better care of yourself during the retirement chapter of your life—reaching age eighty-four is more likely. **If your income has not doubled from sixty to eighty-four, your standard of living is lower, and for many retirees, this is a problem.** Often people do not realize this until it is too late.

So what can be done to help protect income and grow it at a rate that outpaces inflation?

There are many ways to approach this challenge, and you should ask your financial advisor if there's one that may be a good fit for you. From my perspective, dividends are a solid way to grow income since companies distribute a portion of their profits from the business to investors, usually in the form of cold, hard, cash. Though not always, these companies are typically successful and established. Their dividends are a point of pride and offer them a vehicle to reward investors for owning their shares.

As a result, some companies maintain a long track record of paying consistent dividends and even grow those dividends over time. Though the payment of dividends is not guaranteed, companies like Colgate, 3M, Coca-Cola, and Clorox all have a long track record of paying and adding to their dividends. **We call this a *growth of income* (emphasis on "of") strategy.** Returning to our farmer example, dividends paid are like income from the sale of the crops grown on the land, not the sale of the land itself.

We believe *growth of income* is a better strategy rather than

growth for income.

In times of extreme volatility and uncertainty, it's easy to get thrown off your plan. But as we've seen time and again, abandoning a well-constructed plan in favor of an emotional reaction almost always leads to a poor outcome. Therefore, we encourage investors to keep an eye on their investment income, not their portfolio value.

My guess is your real estate agent doesn't call you every fifteen minutes with an update on the value of your home. This would make even the best investors a little cranky, although this is precisely what investors often try to do with the stock market. Using a cell phone and app, the value of your portfolio is only a glance away.

I'd encourage you to look beyond the value of your portfolio. Try flipping to page two or three in your statement and look for the income line (usually dividends paid). Did your income improve last year? Did it stay the same? Did it go down? Hopefully, your income is rising at a rate higher than inflation. Over a long period, this will likely lead to more choices, more opportunities, and greater freedom.

TIME IS MONEY. TREAT IT THAT WAY

As a financial advisor, I'm typically hired by clients to help them manage their resources. Most often, these are financial resources including cash, investments, etc. Sometimes this includes business resources, such as connecting professionals, encouraging action, and providing advice to help make sound decisions.

But there's another resource that I help investors to consider, one that we all have but tend to be terrible at managing. That resource is *time*.

We've discussed time as a major contributing factor when working toward the success of your investment. But it's also a major contributing factor to the success of your life.

Because time is finite (we all have precisely the same number of minutes in the day—1,440 to be exact), it is our single greatest asset. We can't create more of it, and it will continue to disappear if we choose not to use it. As a result, time is even more valuable than money. Ask anyone on their deathbed if they'd rather have $100,000 or another year to enjoy their friends and family, and I'm sure you'll hear the same answer time and again.

Historically, traditional companies sell products and services in exchange for cash, the most common currency. We trade money for a full pantry, warm clothes, and reliable transportation. We've come to expect this type of transaction, and we use software, services, and even financial advisors to help us manage money for products or service-type purchases. But what about the businesses built to capture our most important currency of time?

Today, many companies sell their products in exchange for time and attention. These companies tend to be web-based. Think services like Facebook, Instagram, Google, Netflix, etc. They exchange their product for your time. As a result, for businesses, your attention has become the most valuable currency in Silicon Valley, and the war to collect more of it is fierce.

This results in the exploitation of some of our worst characteristics as humans. Consider the "pull-to-refresh" action in some of these apps. Sometimes we're rewarded with a new post, match, or picture. Sometimes we're not. But this intermittent reward is exactly what hooks people. Feels a lot like a slot machine, doesn't it? There are studies on the chemical reaction that people experience, and yes, it is very much an addiction.

Because attention has become so valuable, apps and services are designed to gather as much of it as possible, regardless of the psychological toll it may take on the user. This has a profound effect on people who may not be keeping track of their time budget. For example, just how much time did you spend on Facebook last week?

Recently I was introduced to the book, *Making Time*, written by two early Google programmers who were instrumental in the creation of Gmail. The authors of the book laid out many examples of how technology rules our lives and our time. They point out all the defaults that come with the devices we have in our pockets, purses, briefcases, at home, on our desks, and yes, even on our wrists. If you think about time as a currency, you begin to change your mindset on how you spend your time, who takes (steals) your time, and how you might invest your time (Zeratsky and Knapp

2018).

So many freely "pay up" with their time wallet, not thinking about time as a currency. How you invest the time in your time wallet is critical. **Managing money can, and should, be applied similarly to how you manage time.** Wealth can be created and saved, but once the time is spent, it's gone forever. So I encourage you to apply some of the same methods we use to manage money to your time currency. Here is a strategy to follow:

- **Take stock of what you have.** Without trying to change anything, merely monitor your time. *Where are you spending it? How much of it is productive? How much of it is spent on leisure? With whom do you spend it?* Track this, and gain insight into where you currently stand.

- **Build out a time budget.** *Ideally, how much sleep would you like to get? Do you want to budget an hour of your time for exercise? What about self-development via reading or taking a class?* The habits we follow and the small things we do every day ultimately define us. Take the time to build out a budget and set an agenda for yourself. This will limit the feeling of being pushed and pulled in different directions all day.

- **Monitor and alter the budget as life changes.** Nothing is set in stone, and life is continually evolving. Your time budget should evolve as well. As you move toward making work a choice, your priorities are likely to change. Without working all day, you'll find an ample amount of new time to budget. But I'll bet the time spent at work results in feelings of productivity, accomplishment, and pride. Remember to find ways to keep these emotional "banks" topped off with revisions to your time budget.

- **Find ways to create more time.** Now I'm not encouraging you to buy a secondhand DeLorean, but there are ways to stretch the time you have available.

There's a well-known quote by American author H. Jackson Brown that goes, "Don't say you don't have enough time. You have exactly the same number of hours per day that were given to Helen Keller, Pasteur, Michelangelo, Mother Teresa, Leonardo da Vinci, Thomas Jefferson, and Albert Einstein."

But I want to challenge the notion that we all have the same amount of time each day. Think about it like this: I doubt Michelangelo had to mow his yard. I bet Thomas Jefferson didn't spend much time in traffic. And when Einstein showed up at the restaurant, they probably made a table available for him.

My point is this: though time is finite, it can still be bought and sold. Millions of Americans sell their time every day, usually in the form of an hourly job. Quite literally, they're paid to sell their time and talents. Likewise, time can and should be bought whenever available. I pay someone to mow my yard, not because I don't know how to work a lawnmower, but because I get to spend time with my family instead of hauling around grass.

This fact was understood by those just discussed. Any time spent away from their unique pursuits was wasted—the equivalent of throwing money down the drain. So, they sought help for those tasks, using their time more effectively and meaningfully in an effort to accomplish what was important to them.

TRADING YOUR WEALTH FOR HEALTH

Time as a resource was deeply ingrained in a former colleague. In 2012, she approached me with the idea of selling her investment firm to me. At the ripe old age of fifty, she was ready to stow away her calculator and unplug her Bloomberg terminal. What I couldn't understand was why someone in her prime, with a healthy list of clients, was interested in walking away from the business. Everything was going great—*why change?*

Her reason was personal. Her husband was twenty years older, and she wanted to spend time with him. In ten years, she feared having to push him around in a wheelchair to see the sites of the world. Why not experience travel while they were still healthy and able? Both were in great physical shape and active cyclists, skiers, and hikers. They wanted to take advantage of it.

Then, things took a turn for the worse. At the ages of fifty-seven and seventy-seven, her husband was diagnosed with a heart condition. He passed shortly thereafter. Now it made sense to me: she'd bought time, and in this example, time was precious. They were able to see the world, travel, explore, and enjoy their relationship. That time was worth more than any amount of money.

You don't have to be wealthy to buy time. You don't need to hire a staff of assistants to pick up your groceries, do the laundry, and tend to the garden. But what little changes can you make to buy some time? Here are four I try to follow.

1. **Avoid the news; avoid social media.** By design, they both steal as much of your time as they can. Checking in on world events now and again or seeing what the kids are up to on Facebook is one thing, but if the first thing you do every morning is reach for your phone, you might have a problem.

2. **Be in control of your time.** Significant income traded for a stressful work environment wears thin. We all have parts of our jobs that are difficult. It's hard to put a price on the value of being in control of what you work on, who you work with, where you work, and whether the work is meaningful. Being part of a team who collaborates, creates, innovates to solve problems, or develops solutions makes work a joy.

3. **Consider your commute.** Early in my career, I had a thirty-minute drive each way. Realizing I'd be investing over five years of my life looking at the dashboard, I re-evaluated where my office was located and moved it to

within five minutes of my house. Buying that time was one of my best investments. This may not be possible for some people, but with modern technology and the uptick in people working from home after COVID-19, working remotely is the new normal.

4. **Surround yourself with meaningful relationships.** Research says people with deep, engaging relationships disproportionately live longer. In the book *The Blue Zones*, author Dan Buettner profiles five parts of the world where a disproportionate number of people live past the age of one hundred. Primarily he attributes this to three things: genetics, lifestyle including diet and stress, and engagement with family, friends, and faith (Buettner 2010). Health, both physically and interpersonally, can help you find additional years of time.

Time is your most valuable asset. And though time is technically finite, there are ways to improve how you spend your time. Take a look at how and where yours is spent, and remember, money is a small price to pay for time with loved ones.

DECIDING ON ENOUGH

At a party given by a billionaire on Shelter Island, the late Kurt Vonnegut informed his friend, author Joseph Heller, that their host, a hedge fund manager, had made more money in a single day than Heller had earned from his wildly popular novel, *Catch-22*, over its entire history.

Author Heller responded, **"Yes, but I have something that he will never have—enough."**

From the book, *Don't Count on It*, by the late John Bogle, this story is a welcome reminder of the dangers of comparison (Bogle 2010). Comparing ourselves to others often leads to feelings of inferiority or regret: there's always a bigger fish in the sea. As President Roosevelt said, "Comparison is the thief of joy."

Yet, comparison tends to be the lens through which most people view their finances. Some people assume wealth is the amount of money you have in the bank or the size of your investment portfolio. Others judge wealth based on the size or neighborhood of their home or the number of cars or toys they have. Some measure wealth based on income.

But my definition of wealth is much broader than the material. People can earn $100k and spend $125k. That's not how wealth is built. Likewise, that same person may spend less than they make but spend 80 hours away from their friends and family working to earn it. Their work may be in a disinteresting field or for a cause in which they have no desire to help. Or they work with people who consume their energy, not encourage and contribute to it.

What determines a wealthy life depends on your relationship

with money and what matters most to you. There are many ways to become rich that don't involve money:

- I believe one of the most valuable measurements of wealth is the ability to control **your time**. The freedom and time to pursue whatever you want is a true measure of your wealth.

- Another is the ability to control **your purpose**—your *why*. Is your work accomplished only for a paycheck? Or do you feel as if you are contributing to something bigger than yourself?

- A third would be **your relationships**—with whom you choose to do things, collaborate, or just spend time.

- Lastly might be **your income**, having enough cash flow to provide for what you want to do, with whom, when, and for how long.

Being content in all things is a rich life. When you are content, a number doesn't matter—your mindset matters.

Money does not make life less stressful. On the contrary, for many, it makes life more stressful. With money comes the need to guard it, protect it, keep it, not lose it, and so on. Money, however, is merely a tool, a resource to provide you the freedom of your endeavors. Hoarding does little good; having your resources serve you works.

Yet, some people are more prone to anxiety than others. No amount of money is enough to quench their thirst or satiate these deeply rooted questions:

- *What if the market crashes and doesn't come back?*
- *What if inflation is much higher than expected?*
- *What if my candidate for the White House doesn't get elected?*
- *What if I lose my job?*
- *What if the economy goes into a terrible recession or a depression?*
- *What if I pick the wrong investments?*
- *What if I'm saving too little or too much?*
- *What if there's another pandemic?*

You can drive yourself crazy chasing away these "what ifs." There will always be something to worry about when investing, planning for your financial future, and building or preserving your wealth. However, the concern should not focus on these particular questions but on learning how to deal with the unknown in a healthy way. If these questions constantly chip away at your confidence, taking up space in your brain, you'll never learn to feel content. As a friend used to say, "Worrying is a poor use of the imagination."

How you think about these things is essential; it is your mindset. Developing a time-specific, income-specific plan that offers ample flexibility is critical, yet most people spend more time planning their vacation than their retirement. A vacation lasts a couple of weeks—a retirement two, three, or four decades. So, it is wise to have a plan.

Nick Murray says it best in *Simple Wealth, Inevitable Wealth,* "No matter how much money you have, if you're still worried, you aren't wealthy" (Murray 2010).

CHAPTER 6

The Wisdom to Make a Difference

WILL YOU MAKE BETTER DECISIONS?

Some people can naturally make wise choices, be disciplined, pursue new knowledge, and have a deep understanding of themselves and the people they surround themselves with. Yet it is rare.

In my career as a financial advisor, I've seen what I believe are some of the most successful people in their businesses making simple, critical, elementary mistakes. I've seen industry transformers fall prey to the emotions of greed and fear.

Your experience in your business does not give you the muscles to be wise with your resources. That's why there is wisdom in having a coach.

A great coach not only knows the athlete—including their limits, weaknesses, strengths, and desired outcome—but also has the right motive. Their skin in the game is for that athlete to compete and win. And win again over and over—meaning *safely* win. Not winning at all costs, but rather with longevity and success of the athlete in mind.

I'll give you an example from one of my clients; let's call him Chuck. Chuck recently sold his business to a partner and was asking my advice on an investment that would permit him to avoid paying capital gains taxes on the sale of his business. I asked questions about his motive, his goals, his experience with financial products that were rooted in generating tax benefits for investors, the control he would have over the investment (lack of liquidity, management, or influence in what would happen with his money), and several other variables. At the end of the conversation, Chuck was able to reflect on what was most important rather than what he was fearing (paying the taxes). At the end of the day, Chuck saw what behavior he was leaning toward, and the potential consequences. Chuck needed advice to guide him toward better choices—*to have the best behavior.*

That is what a coach does.

How will you put into practice the lessons in this book? How will you use these lessons not only to strengthen your investment muscle, but to improve your investor behavior?

We live in a world in which everyone everywhere is selling something. We're thus constantly bombarded with messaging. Usually these messages seek to plant the idea that *whatever you have, whoever you are, or whatever you are doing just isn't good enough. If you'd try this soap, or buy this car, or invest in that condo, you would be that much better as a person.* It takes strong muscles to fight off those messages. It takes a strong focus to remain steadfast in what you are doing.

Doubt is such an easy tool to distract people. But remember, *your attention is your property.* Don't spend it just anywhere. And don't let people, businesses, or trends take it from you. Your attention belongs to you—so protect it.

At times, fighting your emotions will feel like fighting gravity. Like the fish not realizing he's surrounded by water, your emotions make up who you are as a person. They can steer you in new directions, challenge the status quo, or sap your desire to get out of bed in the morning.

Yet the more you recognize your emotions and reconcile them with your long-term goals, both financial and otherwise, the more likely you will be to accomplish them. Understanding your emotions doesn't mean conquering them. It means practicing introspection enough to realize when your approach simply isn't suited for investing. For those situations, utilize a coach who can work for you and with you to seek a better result.

You are your emotions, your behavior, and your future. Improve your investor behavior, and watch it improve your life.

Resources

INVESTMENT EXPERIENCE TOOL   Date: ____/____/_____

Describe the investment.

Why did I make the investment?

What was the outcome?

What worked?

What didn't work?

What did I learn?

What will I do next time?

A printable version of this worksheet is available at blindspotinvesting.com

INVESTMENT FILTER TOOL

Date: ____/_____/_____

What do I hope to achieve with this investment?

What does the ideal outcome look like?

How will I score my experience? (Ideal outcome)	How is this important to my plan? (Your why)

Evaluate
What does this look like as an A+?

What does failure look like?

RETIRE FROM / RETIRE TO TOOL   Date: ____/_____/_____

Time is one of the most valuable assets you can have. Your freedom of time enables you to do what you want to do, when you want to do it, and with whom. Structure your investments such that they give you these freedoms.

Retire From...	Retire To...

In my new life I am going to...

Stop Doing...	Start Doing...

A printable version of this worksheet is available at blindspotinvesting.com

INVESTMENT EVALUATION TOOL   Date: ____/_____/_____

Name of investment:

Structure:

☐ C-Corp. (Qualified dividends, generally lower tax rates, favored)

☐ Partnership (Complex for tax reporting)

☐ REIT (Taxed at ordinary Income tax rates)

Dividend:

Rate _____% (current yield, ideally over 2.5%)

History:

_____/_____% 5/10 year dividend growth rate (Ideally over 6% per year)

_____% recent dividend increase? (Ideally over 4%)

_____dividend payout ratio (% earnings paid out)

Y / N   ever had a dividend cut?

Industry:

☐ "Everybody, everywhere, every day" Industry

Financial Stewardship - When the company does a buyback is it at a:

☐ Low Valuation? (Preferred)

☐ High Valuation? (Not preferred)

Valuation:

_____ Price vs. Earnings (ideally under 15x)

_____ Price vs. Owner Earnings (ideally under 15x)

_____% Earnings Yield (Earnings/Price) (ideally over 6.5%)

_____ Dividend vs. Cash Flow

_____ Dividend vs. Free Cash Flow

Feels like they are: over-distributing, under-distributing, or just right?

Describe their unfair advantage (what makes what they do better than everyone else?):

References

"2021 Investment Company Fact Book." 2021. Investment Company Institute. May 2021. https://www.ici.org/system/files/2021-05/2021_factbook.pdf.

Arends, Brett. 2019. "Americans Spend 7,000% More Time Watching TV than They Do on Their Finances." MarketWatch. October 21, 2019. https://www.marketwatch.com/story/americans-spend-7000-more-time-watching-tv-than-they-do-on-their-finances-2019-10-18.

Browning, E.S. 2010. "Small Investors Flee Stocks, Changing Market Dynamics." The Wall Street Journal. Dow Jones & Company. July 12, 2010. https://www.wsj.com/articles/SB10001424052748704545004575353102793970916.

Buettner, Dan. 2010. The Blue Zones: Lessons for Living Longer from the People Who've Lived the Longest. Washington, DC: National Geographic Society.

Buffett, Warren. Letter to Shareholders of Berkshire Hathaway Inc. 1995. "Chairman's Letter." Berkshire Hathaway, March 1995. https://www.berkshirehathaway.com/letters/1994.html.

Buffett, Warren. Letter to Shareholders of Berkshire Hathaway Inc. 2008. "Chairman's Letter." Berkshire Hathaway, March 2008. https://www.berkshirehathaway.com/letters/2007ltr.pdf.

Carlson, Ben. 2014. "What If You Only Invested at Market Peaks?" A Wealth of Common Sense. February 25, 2014. https://awealthofcommonsense.com/2014/02/worlds-worst-market-timer/.

Carlson, Ben. 2014. "What If You Only Invested at Market Peaks?" A Wealth of Common Sense. February 25, 2014. https://awealthofcommonsense.com/2014/02/worlds-worst-market-timer/.

Cherry, Kendra. 2020. "Why Our Brains Are Hardwired to Focus on the Negative." Verywell Mind. April 29, 2020. https://www.verywellmind.com/negative-bias-4589618.

"Cost-of-Living Adjustment Information for 2022." 2021. SSA. Social Security Administration. December 2021. https://www.ssa.gov/cola/.

Fried, Carla. 2019. "What's Your Retirement Number? No, Not Savings -- Life Expectancy." Rate.com. Guaranteed Rate. June 28, 2019. https://www.rate.com/research/news/retirement-expectancy.

Gladwell, Malcolm. 2019. Outliers: The Story of Success. New York, NY: Back Bay Books, Little, Brown and Company.

"Historical Frequency of Positive Stock Returns." 2018. Fisher 401k. Fisher Investments 401(k) Solutions. February 2018. https://www.fisher401k.com/resource-library/fees/positive-returns.

"How Dangerous Is Lightning?" 2019. National Weather Service. National Oceanic and Atmospheric Association. March 12, 2019. https://www.weather.gov/safety/lightning-odds.

Johnson, Mary. 2019. "Social Security Benefits Lose 33% of Buying Power since 2000." The Senior Citizens League. May 13, 2019. https://seniorsleague.org/loss-of-buying-power-2/.

Kahneman, Daniel, and Amos Tversky. 1979. "On the Interpretation of Intuitive Probability: A Reply to Jonathan Cohen." Cognition 7 (4): 409–11. https://doi.org/10.1016/0010-0277(79)90024-6.

Kahneman, Daniel, and Amos Tversky. 1979. "Prospect Theory: An Analysis of Decision under Risk." Econometrica 47 (2): 263. https://doi.org/10.2307/1914185.

Kaplan, Elle. 2017. "Why Warren Buffett's '20-Slot Rule' Will Make You Insanely Successful and Wealthy." CNBC. NBC. March 16, 2017. https://www.cnbc.com/2017/03/16/warren-buffetts-20-slot-rule-will-make-you-successful-and-wealthy.html.

Langley, Karen. 2020. "Dividend Payouts Are Poised to Top $500 Billion for the First Time This Year." The Wall Street Journal. Dow Jones & Company. January 9, 2020. https://www.wsj.com/articles/dividend-payouts-are-poised-to-top-500-billion-for-the-first-time-this-year-11578599555.

Lee, Chaiwoo, and Joseph F. Coughlin. 2018. "Describing Life after Career: Demographic Differences in the Language and Imagery of Retirement." Financial Planning Association. AARP. August 1, 2018. https://www.financialplanningassociation.org/article/journal/AUG18-describing-life-after-career-demographic-differences-language-and-imagery-retirement.

Lynch, Peter, and John Rothchild. 1995. "Fear of Crashing." Worth, September 1995.

"Market Insights Investment Outlook 2022." 2021. J.P. Morgan Asset Management. J.P. Morgan Chase. 2021. https://am.jpmorgan.com/content/dam/jpm-am-aem/global/en/insights/market-insights/mi-investment-outlook-ce-en.pdf.

"Mosquito-Borne Diseases." n.d. American Mosquito Control Association. Accessed December 20, 2021. https://www. mosquito.org/general/custom.asp?page=diseases.

Murray, Nick. 2019. Simple Wealth, Inevitable Wealth. Nick Murray Company, Inc.

Neuman, Scott. 2017. "Nobel Goes to American Richard Thaler for Work in Behavioral Economics." NPR. October 9, 2017. https://www.npr.org/sections/thetwo-way/2017/10/09/556610760/nobel-goes-to-american-richard-thaler-for-work-in-behavioral-economics.

"Planning and Progress Study 2019." 2019. Northwestern Mutual. 2019. https://news.northwesternmutual.com/planning-and-progress-2019.

Pound, Jesse. 2020. "Legendary Investor Stanley Druckenmiller Says He Doesn't like the Way the Market Is Set Up." CNBC. NBC. May 12, 2020. https://www.cnbc.com/2020/05/12/risk-reward-for-stocks-is-maybe-as-bad-as-ive-seen-it-stanley-druckenmiller-says.html.

Ropeik, David. 2006. "How Risky Is Flying?" PBS. Public Broadcasting Service. September 2006. https://www.pbs.org/wgbh/nova/planecrash/risky.html.

Roser, Max. 2020. "The Short History of Global Living Conditions and Why It Matters That We Know It." Our World in Data. Oxford Martin School. 2020. https://ourworldindata.org/a-history-of-global-living-conditions-in-5-charts.

Rosling, Hans, Ola Rosling, and Rönnlund Anna Rosling. 2020. Factfulness: Ten Reasons We're Wrong about the World - and Why Things Are Better than You Think. New York, NY: Flatiron Books.

Ryan, Richard M., and Edward L. Deci. 2000. "Self-Determination Theory and the Facilitation of Intrinsic Motivation, Social Development, and Well-Being." American Psychologist 55 (1): 68–78. https://doi.org/10.1037/0003-066x.55.1.68.

"The S&P 500 at Your Fingertips." 2006. Political Calculations. December 6, 2006. https://politicalcalculations. blogspot.com/2006/12/sp-500-at-your-fingertips.html#. YcNfZ1lOk2w.

Thaler, Richard H. 2016. Misbehaving: the Making of Behavioral Economics. New York, NY: W.W. Norton & Company.

Tversky, Amos, and Daniel Kahneman. 1992. "Advances in Prospect Theory: Cumulative Representation of Uncertainty." Journal of Risk and Uncertainty 5 (4): 297–323. https://doi. org/10.1007/bf00122574.

"United States Inflation Rate: 1914-2020 Historical." 2021. Trading Economics. 2021. https://tradingeconomics.com/united-states/inflation-cpi.

Zeratsky, John, and Jake Knapp. 2018. Make Time: How to Focus on What Matters Every Day. London: Bantam Press.

About Steve Booren

STEVE BOOREN

Owner/Founder
Prosperion Financial Advisors
LPL Financial Advisor

Phone: (303) 793-3202
Email: steve.booren@lpl.com
Web: www.prosperion.us
Mailing Address:
8400 E. Prentice Ave.
Suite 1125
Greenwood Village, CO 80111

Steve Booren started his investment career in 1978 with a NYSE investment firm. To provide clients with objective investment advice, he started Prosperion Financial Advisors in 1996, working to identify clients' opportunities and strengths and to develop strategies to manage risk. Steve is an avid cycler, accomplished skier, mediocre golfer and happy grandfather. With his wife Marie, he has two married children, Scott and John.

ALSO BY STEVE BOOREN

Intelligent Investing

Your Guide to a Growing Retirement Income

In his book, Intelligent Investing: Your Guide to a Growing Retirement Income, author Steve Booren helps to prove that no matter who you are or what your retirement goals are, the more you know, the better the decisions you'll make.

CPSIA information can be obtained
at www.ICGtesting.com
Printed in the USA
JSHW011539150223
37714JS00005B/21